FOIL FENCING

About the Author

Muriel Bower earned her B.S. degree from the University of California at Los Angeles, her M.A. degree from the University of Southern California, and the Master of Arms degree from the United States Fencing Coaches Association.

She was a nationally ranked fencer during her competitive years and has taught and coached fencing to both men and women for more than thirty years, during which time her students have often gained regional and national distinction.

Mrs. Bower is past chairwoman of the National Collegiate Athletic Association Fencing Committees for both men and women. She served a term as chairwoman of the United States Collegiate Sports Council Fencing Committee. She acted as a special official to the 1964 Olympic fencing events in Tokyo, was manager of the women's fencing team at the World University Games in Russia in 1973, and served in protocol for fencing events during the 1984 Olympic Games in Los Angeles.

Mrs. Bower served as West Coast vice-president of the United States Fencing Coaches Association for two terms of office. She also held the office of president of the Western Regional Intercollegiate Fencing Championships and served as Commissioner for this Association for many years.

Mrs. Bower is a member of the U.S. Fencing Coaches Association and of the U.S. Fencing Association.

FOIL FENCING

Eighth Edition

Muriel Bower
Commissioner, Western Regional Intercollegiate Fencing Conference

Brown & Benchmark
PUBLISHERS

Madison, WI Dubuque Guilford, CT Chicago Toronto London
Mexico City Caracas Buenos Aires Madrid Bogotá Sydney

Book Team

Executive Managing Editor *Ed Bartell*
Project Editor *Theresa Grutz*
Production Editor *Ann Morgan*
Proofreading Coordinator *Carrie Barker*
Art Editor *Rita Hingtgen*
Photo Editor *Leslie Dague*
Production Manager *Beth Kundert*
Production/Imaging and Media Development Manager *Linda Meehan Avenarius*
Production/Costing Manager *Sherry Padden*
Visuals/Design Freelance Specialist *Mary L. Christianson*
Senior Marketing Manager *Pamela S. Cooper*
Copywriter *Sandy Hyde*

Basal Text *10/12 Times Roman*
Display Type *Helvetica*
Typesetting System *Macintosh*™
  QuarkXpress™
Paper Stock *70# Restore Cote*

Brown & Benchmark
PUBLISHERS

Executive Vice President and General Manager *Bob McLaughlin*
Vice President of Business Development *Russ Domeyer*
Vice President of Production and New Media Development *Victoria Putman*
National Sales Manager *Phil Rudder*
National Telesales Director *John Finn*

 A Times Mirror Company

PE Series
Consulting Editor *Aileene Lockhart, Texas Women's University*

Cover photograph © *Joe McBride/Tony Stone Images*

Copyedited by *Rose R. Kramer*

Proofread by *Nancy Phan*

Library of Congress Catalog Card Number: 95–83965

ISBN 0–697–25874–2

Printed in the United States of America by Times Mirror Higher Education Group, Inc.,
2460 Kerper Boulevard, Dubuque, IA 52001

10 9 8 7 6 5 4 3 2 1

Contents

Psychological and Physical Conditioning for Fencing 67

6

Bouting for the More Advanced Fencer 75

7

Rules of Fencing 85

8

The Language of Fencing—
A Glossary 103

9

Preface

This eighth edition of *Foil Fencing* has been written specifically as a source of information for all who are learning fencing. Its usefulness extends from an introduction to fencing to more advanced levels. Standard (nonelectric) fencing techniques and rules that are appropriate for beginning fencers are presented as is information for the more advanced, electrically scored fencing techniques and rules.

My aim is to present a concise, inexpensive book to augment fencing lessons, but the book may well be useful to any student of fencing. Tactics are presented throughout the book in the form of examples of when to use various actions and what the probable reactions will be. While not intended as an exhaustive treatise on all possible actions and reactions, these are suggestions upon which a thoughtful fencer can expand to build a game and set overall strategy. It is my hope that the general area of tactics will be understood rather than memorized, because only in this way can learners become thinking fencers with an adaptable and expanding game.

Chapters are presented in the order in which the material is likely to be used. After the introductory chapters 1 and 2, chapter 3 presents basic techniques, followed by what to expect when first starting to bout in chapter 4. After this more advanced techniques and bouting are discussed in chapter 5.

While information regarding physical and mental preparation for bouting will be useful to developing fencers, my desire was to present fencing techniques first, so chapter 6 addresses aspects of training. Information that is presented in this book certainly does not have to be used in exactly the order it is presented but the progression of techniques presented here is a useful one from an author's standpoint. When fencing techniques can be demonstrated as they are explained, a somewhat different progression may be more practical.

I hope that material in later chapters will be used along with the critical, basic information in chapters 3 through 5.

Material presented in this book is current in terms of what is happening today in fencing. There have been several rule changes in the past few years and these are included in this book.

The test at the back of the book is intended as a study guide.

It is my hope that readers of this book will find the sport of fencing to be an exciting, invigorating activity. Rewards from this stimulating sport may well last a lifetime!

What Is Fencing?

1

Fencing is the historic art of offense and defense with the sword. Throughout human history the way of fighting with weapons has been closely tied to the ability to fashion tools of warfare. Primitive people engaged in a crude form of fencing as they attempted to bludgeon opponents with clubs. As metal came into general use, broad, metal blades of many kinds and shapes were used in battle.

Early Fencing

In ancient times, gladiators were taught the art of sword fighting. They used short, double-edged hacking and cutting swords with a shield or buckler for protection from an opponent's blade. Later, some double-edged swords were several feet long, requiring both hands to wield such ungainly weapons. Such broadswords were not commonly used for protection, although attacks were sometimes met with the base of the hilt. Blows made with heavy broadswords would have taken incredible arm strength if a defender tried to stop an attack with his blade and, in all likelihood, at least one of the blades would have broken on impact since they were not well tempered. Combatants relied instead on their ability to sidestep (and thus avoid the slow blade attacks), and on bucklers or shields for defense.

By the twelfth century early knights wore chain mail as protection against slashing attacks. When thinner, longer blades were developed that could penetrate the chain mail, plate armor was worn for protection against broadswords and lances. Swords were again made to be heavy as slashing actions were more effective against the armor and slow attacks met with slow defenses. If an unlucky duelist was unhorsed or tripped and fell he was as much at the mercy of his opponent as an upturned turtle and could be easily dispatched with his opponent's sword or dagger. The dagger thus became a useful second sword because at close range it could penetrate between "chinks" in an opponent's armor.

Refinement of swords and the imperfect protection that plate armor afforded, especially against gunshot, led to the discarding of such armor in the sixteenth century.[1]

Mobility was greatly increased once the heavy armor was in disuse, and the lighter, thinner, one-handed thrusting swords, or rapiers, developed. Now that the back hand was not needed, the body was turned sideways to present a narrow target, although the back hand occasionally held a dagger for defense in infighting until the eighteenth century.[2] Defense continued to rely on the use of daggers, cloaks, and agility for many years before the system of parrying with the blade came into general use.

During the sixteenth century the first generation of fencing masters arose, professing to teach the art of swordsmanship on an allegedly scientific basis.[3] For a price, fencing masters taught secret thrusts to duelists. The lunge is attributed to Carnello Aguppa in the early seventeenth century.[4] According to Aldo Nadi, one of the greatest modern fencers, it was the Italian master, Angelo, who developed a circular parry and probably the riposte,[5] both of which are discussed in chapter 3.

Fencing developed into a true, invigorating sport in the seventeenth century when gunpowder and firearms replaced the sword as the basic weapon. Swordsmanship developed into a sport in which the objective became to touch and not to injure or kill. Today much of the excitement and romance of serious dueling remain as fencers attempt to defend against an opponent's point while at the same time trying to find an opening in the opponent's defense.

Masks made of wire and tied on with string are said to have been invented by La Boessiere, a French fencing master, about the middle of the eighteenth century, but they were not in common use until the end of that century.[6]

Fencing Today

Fencing actions are now much faster than they were in the past and require more refinement of technique than was possible with the heavier, longer, and stiffer weapons used by the early fencer.

Modern fencing has become a safe sport due to the protective clothing and flexible, blunted blade that are used while fencing. The objective of fencing is not to inflict an injury but to demonstrate an ability to outmaneuver an opponent and to score.

Fencing Etiquette

During the so-called Age of Chivalry in the sixteenth century, the popularity of dueling went hand in hand with the development of fencing into a fine art as fencers realized the necessity of improving their skill. The rapier became a gentleman's badge, worn only by nobility who practiced to become adept in its use. Noblewomen also studied fencing, and there are recorded instances of duels between women. The courtesies of fencing practice and of dueling were elaborate and precise, in keeping with the elevated station of the participants.

Fencing etiquette today reflects the general spirit that prevailed in the days of dueling. Fencing is still a sport for people who conduct themselves as ladies and gentlemen, and the accepted standards of fencing conduct are universal.

Until the early twentieth century, fencing form and sportsmanship were considered as important as scoring. Tournaments were judged on the basis of form, much as gymnastics is judged today. The manner in which one made an attack or defense was as important as whether or not it succeeded. Fencers were required to acknowledge touches against themselves and were penalized if judges saw a touch that was not called by the person who was touched.

Today the criterion on which a fencer is judged is the more realistic one of whether or not a point lands; however, poor sportsmanship and unnecessary roughness can still cost a fencer points.

The comprehensive written and unwritten laws of etiquette are taught and adhered to in all reputable fencing centers throughout the world. The rules and manner of fencing reflect its original purpose even though techniques and tactics have undergone many changes through the years. There are three weapons used in fencing today: the foil, the epee, and the sabre. For many years women competed only in foil, but today many fencers of both sexes enjoy competing in all three weapons.

Foil

The foil was designed as a practice weapon so duelists could safely train, and it is the weapon with which this book is concerned. It is the first weapon that is commonly taught because it is considered basic to fencing. This does not mean that the foil is merely a beginner's weapon to be discarded once a person becomes proficient in its use; it is probably the most difficult of the three weapons to master and offers a lifelong challenge to men and women alike. Once a fencer learns to use the foil well, he or she can readily learn to use the sabre and epee.

Although the foil is blunted, it is theoretically a pointed sword capable of inflicting only a puncture wound. A touch is scored if the point of the blade hits any part of the valid target area, which is limited to the torso, from the collar to the groin lines in front, and on the back and sides from the collar to the hips. If the point lands anywhere else, it is "off target" and is not valid. In foil, only those touches that would be potentially fatal in serious dueling are counted. There is no penalty for an off-target hit. Any point hit, valid or not, stops action, and no subsequent touches count until the fencers have stopped and once more resumed fencing. A bout ends when a fencer has scored five times.

In foil fencing a definite sequence of action should be followed. In such a *phrase d'armes,* a well-executed attack, initiated by one fencer, must be parried (defended against) or evaded before the defender can safely riposte (take the offense). This is a logical sequence of action when you consider that if someone were coming toward you with a sharp sword, your first consideration would be to defend yourself and then to hit in return. It would be dangerous to attack into an attacker with a sharp sword because both fencers could be wounded or killed, so the rules do not favor this type of play.

Sabre

The sabre is oriental in origin. From the sixteenth to the eighteenth centuries Turks raided their border countries on fast ponies using their curved sabres, which were

Figure 1.1
Weapons: sabre, epee, foil with a pistol grip, electric foil with a French grip.

very effective slicing or thrusting weapons. The Poles, Hungarians, and Austrians resorted to the use of sabres of their own design to combat the marauders.[7]

Today's sabre has a light, flexible blade that may be used as a thrusting or cutting weapon. Although the sabre blade has a theoretical cutting edge, rules now permit cuts to be made with any part of the blade.

Touches are scored on the upper part of the body above a horizontal line drawn through the highest points of intersection of the thighs and trunk of the fencer when in the on-guard position.

Sabre rules concerning who has the right to attack (right-of-way) are similar to those governing foil in that the well-executed attack must be parried before a riposte is made. The sabre target is larger than that of the foil since the arms and head are also valid targets, so there is a greater variety of actions possible than in foil. Movements are often larger than those of foil due to the enlarged target area and the cutting attacks common in sabre, but precise control is just as vital here as in the other weapons.

Epee

Epee more closely resembles real dueling than any other weapon. The epee, or dueling sword, is stiffer and heavier than the foil, but it is a point, or thrusting, weapon. Touches anywhere on the body are valid, and no definite sequence of play must be followed. The first person to hit scores. If two fencers hit simultaneously, both are declared touched.

Electrical Scoring

In keeping with this electronic age, all three weapons must now be electrically scored in official meets, with sabre being the most recent weapon to be scored electrically.

Due to the difficulty in accurately judging touches by sight, an electrical scoring system for epee was developed many years ago. The foil scoring machine was first used for a major international tournament in the 1955 World Championship meet.

Electrical epees and foils have a button at the tip that is depressed when a touch is made and indicates the touch by means of a light and buzzer on a central scoring machine. In electrical epee, only a simple circuit is needed since a point may land anywhere on the body. In foil, however, the problem is complicated by the limited, valid target area and by the possibility of off-target hits. The electrical foil scoring machine was developed more slowly than the epee machine because it has to differentiate between fair and foul touches. Over the regular jacket, foil fencers wear a metallic vest that covers only the valid target area. The machine registers with a colored light if the point lands on the valid area and a white light if the point lands anywhere off target.

The technology for scoring sabre developed much later because scoring cuts as well as thrusts electrically on a limited target posed special problems. Because the valid sabre target includes the mask, arms, and hands, practical ways to electrically activate those areas had to be perfected. The first electrically scored sabre tournament in the United States took place in March of 1986, and electrical scoring is currently required in all official sabre tournaments.

Values of Fencing

Fencing is a vigorous sport that requires and develops stamina, quick reactions, speed and accuracy of movement, and excellent coordination.

Fencing is also a mental game. Once a fencer has practiced the various movements until physically able to carry out a plan without having to think about how the various parts of the body must move, the real excitement lies in outthinking and outwitting the opponent. The fencer must quickly analyze an adversary's style and then plan strategy accordingly. Traps must be set for the opponent while being careful to avoid those set by the other fencer.

In addition to the need for a keen, analytical mind, fencing requires decisive thinking and the courage to assume the offensive at any instant that an opportunity arises. If a fencer delays in building up the courage to move, the exact moment will be lost. On the other hand, a fencer may increase self-confidence by forcefully dominating an opponent while successfully carrying out planned attacks.

Figure 1.2
Electric scoring machine and reels. Reel (A); scoring machine (B); body cord attachment (C).
(Photo by David Cary)

Good sportsmanship is an integral part of fencing tradition. For many years fencing was considered a sport for gentlemen and ladies only, and participants were expected to conduct themselves accordingly. Much of this flavor still exists. A pleasant outcome is the comaraderie that tends to develop between fencers who regularly compete against each other.

Safety

Fencing is one of the safest sports if simple precautions are observed. It is always a mistake to cross blades with anyone unless each person is wearing the mask and jacket that protect the body, the foil arm, and the neck. Accidents can very easily happen to the unprotected fencer because a fencer can be responsible only for his or her own actions. Once a second person is involved, you cannot know exactly how the opponent will move or react, and a fencer is apt to react reflexively to a fast-moving blade in such a way as to endanger an unprotected person.

The fencing jacket must be fully buttoned in order to properly protect the neck and torso. Holes should be mended. The mask must have a thick bib to protect the throat, and the wire mesh of the mask must not show spots of rust where a blade could penetrate. Dents in the mask should be carefully removed. (See chapter 2 for further safety precautions regarding the uniform.)

Figure 1.3
Fencer hooked to reel. Ground wire is hooked to lamé vest at left of reel attachment.

Figure 1.4
Fencers wearing regulation uniforms for electrical fencing. Note reel cord at back of fencers.

The standard (nonelectric) foil tip should be examined frequently to see that it is covered by a rubber button or a strip of adhesive tape one-fourth inch wide and four inches long that must be wrapped around it. If even a small portion of a blade breaks, it must be discarded. Under no circumstances should it ever be retaped and used because a measure of flexibility is lost, and a jagged end remains that could easily cause serious damage. Blades can be replaced by unscrewing the pommel, removing the handle and guard, and putting a new blade in the old mounting.

Pants that cover the upper leg should be worn rather than shorts. It is very dangerous to fence in shorts, because a blade may end up inside the leg of the shorts and inflict painful groin injuries. There should be no gap between the lower portion of the jacket and the top of the trousers when the fencer is on guard. In short, all parts that could be hit should be protected.

Fencing Schools

In the seventeenth century the need for fencing instruction increased as the popularity of dueling grew among the aristocracy. The most important fencing schools originated in Italy, France, and Spain. Each used a different system, and each was considered to be superior by its proponents. The Italian and French systems of fencing proved to be the most widely accepted through the years, and today the influences of these two schools can still be seen. Modifications throughout the years have brought the Italian method, which relied more on power, and the French method, which relied more on finesse, closer together; now the major difference between them is in the shape of the foil handle, which affects the use of the foil.

In this book the French foil is the weapon considered. Although any handle can be used in a similar way, the French handle calls for more finesse and control and is the more balanced foil, making it less tiring to hold. The other grips tend to be more powerful but have a shorter, lighter handle making the weapon point-heavy and thus more fatiguing to hold. Some fencers have strapped these shorter grips to their wrists for added support, but this limits freedom and finesse of movement.

Where to Find Fencing

In Europe fencing traditionally has been a major sport and still is today. Western Europeans have been consistent winners in international tournaments. Although Poland, Hungary, and Russia dominated the field for several years, the Western Europeans are again taking their share of international medals.

In America, fencing is a rapidly growing sport with more and more active participants each year. There are fencing clubs and *salles* in every major city in the United States where men, women, and children can learn to fence and continue to practice. Fencing is receiving additional impetus through efforts of the American Alliance for Health, Physical Education, Recreation, and Dance, which is sponsoring a Lifetime Sport Education Project aimed at increasing national participation in sports such as fencing that may be enjoyed throughout life.

An ever-increasing number of colleges and high schools are offering fencing as more people are becoming involved in this fascinating sport.

There are many sources of information on fencing. You may find active fencing groups in your community through colleges and universities, the YMCA, YWCA, recreation centers, athletic clubs, or telephone directories, which may list fencing schools.

Conduct of the Spectators

The audience at a fencing tournament acts similarly to that at a tennis match. Spectators must not try to influence officials or instruct contestants in any way, although they may applaud a well-executed attack. Quiet is usually necessary so that fencers can hear the commands of the referee and so that their attention will not be unduly diverted by excessive noise. The referee can demand silence, or in extreme situations, may exclude members of the audience, or even coaches, who do not conform to these standards.

How to Knowledgeably Watch a Fencing Bout

In order to follow the action during a bout, a spectator should select one fencer to watch. Try to determine why that person attacked at a particular time. What was the distance? How was the trap, if any, baited to draw the other person's reaction? By identifying with one person it is easier to watch the action develop. Later, you may try to analyze action along with the referee. Who made the attack? Was it parried or otherwise prevented from arriving? See if you are usually in agreement with the referee. This is an excellent way to practice directing techniques if you are learning that skill.

Fencing can be an exciting sport to watch critically, but your interest will soon lag if you do not understand what is happening. Read up on the basics of the sport and become familiar with its terminology if you plan to watch fencing bouts, and certainly if you plan to participate.

United States Fencing Association

In 1891 the Amateur Fencers League of America (AFLA) was founded in New York City. This organization was the official governing body for fencing in the country and was sanctioned by the Federation Internationale d'Escrime (F.I.E.), the international governing body of all amateur fencing. The AFLA was renamed the United States Fencing Association (USFA) in 1981.

Classification of Fencers

Fencers are classified by the USFA according to their tournament performance. Classifications range from A to E, with A being the highest rank. Fencers who have not qualified for a ranking, either because they have not placed high enough in qualifying tournaments or because they are new to fencing, are listed as "Unclassified" fencers. A fencer may fence in any tournament that is specified as that fencer's classification or higher. One may not compete in a meet designated as a lower classification than the designation held by oneself. This system offers ample opportunity for less experienced fencers to compete against outstanding opponents, but it also allows them a chance to win on their own level.

College Fencing in America

Collegiate fencing has been increasing in quality, if not in quantity. Many schools on the East and West Coasts have active competitive schedules, and there is a great deal of fencing throughout the Midwest as well. It is becoming increasingly popular in the South and Southwest. For many schools competition begins in the fall and continues through to spring.

Women's championships are held in various parts of the country in the spring. The oldest such event is the Intercollegiate Women's Fencing Association Championship, which is held in April on the East Coast. In 1971 this organization added the word "national" to its title, becoming the NIWFA, which offered the first national women's collegiate championships.

The men's and women's collegiate competitive seasons are climaxed by regional championships throughout the country at which fencers may qualify to go to the National Collegiate Athletic Association (NCAA) national fencing championships.

Although men's and women's collegiate national championships were originally held at separate sites, for the last several years they have been held consecutively in March at the same school.

International Fencing

All international fencing falls under the jurisdiction of the Federation Internationale d'Escrime (F.I.E.), with which the USFA is affiliated. United States fencers have gained much international prestige over the years. Although this country has not won any Olympic fencing events, it has had finalists and medalists in every weapon. Miguel A. de Capriles served as president of the FIE from 1961–1965, the first and only American to be so honored.

Evaluation Question

Observation of competitive fencing events can be helpful in improving one's own skills. Explore in your area the opportunities to watch club, NCAA, and NIFA competitions.

Notes

1. Eduard Wagner, *Cut and Thrust Weapons* (London: The Hamlin Publishing Group Lmt., 1967), 41.
2. Domenico and Harry Angelo, *The School of Fencing* (reprint, New York: Lands End Press, 1971), 87.
3. E. D. Morton, *A–Z of Fencing* (London: Macdonald Queen Anne Press, 1990), Preface.
4. Wagner, *Cut and Thrust Weapons*, 41.
5. Aldo Nadi, *On Fencing* (New York: G. P. Putnam's Sons, 1943), 20.
6. Morton, *A–Z of Fencing*, 116.
7. Wagner, *Cut and Thrust Weapons*, 116.

Suggested Readings

Barbasetti, Luigi. *The Art of the Foil, With a Short History of Fencing.* New York: E. P. Dutton, 1932.

Cass, Eleanor Baldwin. *The Book of Fencing.* New York: Lothrop, Lee and Shephard Co., 1930.

Moekle, C. "Touché." *American Health* 8, no. 41 (Jan/Feb 1989).

Palffy-Alpar, Julius. *Sword and Masque.* Philadelphia: F. A. Davis Co., 1967.

Selection and Care of Equipment

2

Fencing equipment is relatively inexpensive and with care should last for many years. Although many schools furnish the clothing and equipment needed, anyone who seriously wants to fence should invest in his or her own personal equipment. All necessary clothing and equipment can be purchased from most fencing *salles* or clubs. Any school or fencing group can advise you regarding your fencing needs.

Jacket

The jacket is a vital part of your uniform and should be of good quality. Any manufacturer of fencing clothing must adhere to the minimum safety standards that are required by the rules. Half-jackets or plastrons can be purchased at less cost than a full jacket, but since these could never be used in a tournament and do not afford full protection, they are not a good buy for an individual who cares enough about fencing to invest in clothing. The jacket must be white or of a single pastel color. It may be made of duck, canvas, gabardine, or synthetic stretch fabrics. Duck and canvas are inexpensive and durable. Gabardine is also serviceable, comfortable, and looks somewhat nicer than duck and canvas. It should not be used for epee since it will tear more easily because epee blades are heavier and less flexible than foil or sabre blades.

Stretch fabrics make the most comfortable and best-fitting jackets and trousers, but are somewhat more expensive than the above fabrics. Kevlar is by far the most expensive uniform material and tends to be hot, but due to the safety factor this new material is now required in world championship competitions. Kevlar is a fabric that has been used in spacesuits and has become popular because it is nearly impenetrable and prevents puncture wounds that can occur when a blade breaks. An American-made "ballistic" fabric of similar qualities is also available. Puncture injuries are fairly rare, but all safety precautions are indeed welcome.

Extra padding is required on the front, fencing side, and upper sleeve of jackets. In addition, women are required to wear breast protectors of a rigid material no matter what fabric is used.

The jacket should fit as snugly as possible without restricting movement. If a jacket is too large, loose cloth will make it easier for a point to catch on the fabric for a score. Left-handed fencers should buy jackets that fasten on the right side and are padded on the left.

Underarm Protection

Fencers are required to wear an undergarment that is seamless at the armpit. It must have at least a double thickness in addition to a jacket. This must be a separate piece of clothing and must protect the upper arm, armpit, and fencing side of the body.

Trousers

According to the rules, fencing trousers must be white or of a single pastel color, and must fasten below the knees. While it is best to wear regulation trousers that are lightly padded on top of the leading thigh, you may begin fencing with any light-colored trousers that will allow freedom of movement and will protect the legs. Later you can purchase fencing knickers, which match the jacket, allow for a maximum of motion, resist tearing, and look neat. For safety's sake, however, make sure that there is no gap between the bottom of your jacket and trouser top. Fencing rules require a four inch (100 cm) overlap of jacket and trousers when in the fencing position.

Glove

A glove must be worn on the sword hand to protect the hand of the fencer. A regulation foil glove should be of soft leather with a cuff that completely covers the lower part of the jacket sleeve. It is important for the gauntlet of the glove to cover the end of the sleeve when the arm is fully extended to prevent the opponent's blade from entering the sleeve and perhaps causing an injury. The glove may be lightly padded on the back for extra protection. There may also be a double thickness of leather on the end of the thumb and at the base of the thumb where the most wear occurs.

Foil

The foil consists of the blade and the hilt. The steel, quadrangular blade has three sections: the forte, or the strongest third of the blade; the middle third; and the feeble, or weakest, most flexible third of the blade. The maximum length of the foil blade is 90 centimeters.

The hilt consists of the guard, thumb pad, handle, and pommel. The guard is sometimes referred to as a "bellguard," or just "bell," because of its shape. The thumb pad protects the knuckle of the forefinger from injury in case two fencers hit guards together while infighting. The pad also covers and protects the connecting wire on electric foils.

The handle may be a relatively straight, simple, French style, or one of several varieties of so-called "orthopedic" grips that are molded to the hand in one way or

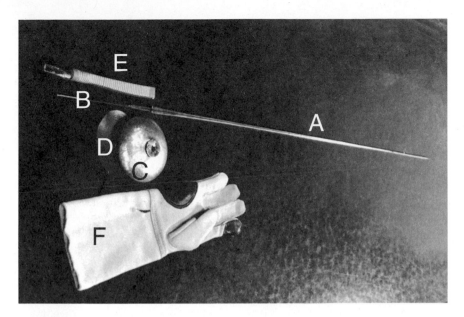

Figure 2.1
Disassembled foil. Blade (A); tang (B); guard (C); thumb pad (D); handle and pommel
(E); glove (F). (Photo by David Cary)

another. French handles are usually made of wood that is wrapped with either cord
or leather. Leather costs a little more but is more durable and tends to slip less in
the hand than cord handles do.

The pommel is the weighted counterbalance at the back end of the foil. It is
threaded to screw onto the tang (the portion of the blade that fits into the handle),
thus holding the complete assembly together.

When selecting a foil, you should pick one that is neither too heavy and inflex-
ible nor too light and whippy. The blade should bend readily, or else it may break
too easily. On the other hand, if the blade is overly flexible the point will be difficult to control.

Blades occasionally break. When this happens, the broken blade can easily be
replaced by unscrewing the pommel, sliding the handle and guard off, and in-
stalling a new one.

If you are more advanced and feel ready to work with electric foils, you
should practice either with an electric foil or with a dummy electric blade. The latter is weighted the same as the electric foil but is less expensive because there is
no wiring. The dummy blade can readily be put into a standard mounting when
you are ready to graduate to electric fencing. It is a mistake to practice with a light
standard foil if you intend to fence with the electric blade in competition; you will
lose accuracy when you switch from a light to a heavier weapon and you will tire
more easily if you do not train with the extra weight. Every fencer should have
two foils, so that if one breaks there is a spare.

Mask

A mask of good quality is an absolute necessity for safety's sake. A new, medium-weight mask will be adequate since the manufacturers must conform to strict standards. The mask should be white or of a light color as specified in the rule book. The prices of masks vary somewhat, but this is partly because of the various trims used on them. Masks with plastic or canvas trim are the least expensive and will serve quite well. Leather trim is more costly, more durable, and looks a little better, but is not necessary. Plastic interior trim is the easiest to keep clean, but it is not quite as comfortable to wear as cloth. In any case, the bib should contain several thicknesses of material to protect the neck. The mask should feel comfortable to the wearer and be secure.

If a person wishes to fence epee or sabre as well as foil, there are three-weapon masks that have a heavier mesh and afford more protection for the top and back of the head.

Whenever any rust appears on a mask, it should be discarded for safety reasons. A mask that has been weakened by rust may be pierced by a heavy hit, and this could result in a severe injury to the fencer. For this reason it is unwise to buy a used mask. A mask is a personal item that you will want to keep for your own use.

Electric Equipment

If you decide to purchase the items necessary for electric foil fencing, you will need at least one, and preferably two, electric foils and at least two body cords. When you enter any electric tournament, you will be required to have two weapons and body cords in working condition.

Wires used in the electric foil are relatively fine and do break occasionally. An armorer is an expert on maintenance and repair of electric equipment and will advise you. An armorer is required at every major tournament. Most fencers learn to make at least minor repairs on their equipment. Fencers can rewire their own blades, repair sockets, and adjust or replace points.

A metallic vest is needed for electric foil fencing. There must not be any tears in this vest, and it must fit so that it exactly corresponds to the valid target. It should be lined to insulate a perspiring fencer against receiving a mild shock when scored against.

Care of Equipment

Fencing clothing will last longer and look better if it is kept clean. Jackets and gloves should be stored so that they will dry after they have been used.

Masks also should be kept clean and dry. The bib can be scrubbed without harming the mask if it is well dried after scrubbing. Never immerse the entire mask in water.

Foils should be stored in a dry place to prevent the formation of rust. They may be hung, point down, or stored so that they rest on the pommel, but they should never rest on the point.

Fencing equipment bags are available for carrying equipment, but if your wet clothing, mask, and foil are all left rolled together after you have used them, the clothing will mildew and the metal objects will soon rust. Transport equipment in the bags, but remove it for permanent storage unless it is dry. With reasonable care, your fencing equipment should last for many years.

Evaluation Question

What piece of equipment should be one of your first purchases? Why should it be bought new, and how should you care for it.

Skills Basic to Fencing

3

A fencing bout between two persons should proceed in an orderly fashion. Either fencer may begin an attack, thereby taking *right-of-way.* The other fencer must defend against the attack at which time the defender may take the offense. The attack following a defense is called a *riposte,* which must be defended against in turn, and so on. The defense made with the blade is called a *parry.* The bout, then, is made up of a series of attacks, parries, ripostes, and counter ripostes until one fencer scores a touch, all of which will be explained in more detail later in this chapter.

Fencing positions are unlike those of any other sport. It is essential that the beginner take the time necessary to practice the basic moves until they become automatic. Then the mind can be free to think in terms of acting and reacting to a second, often unpredictable, person.

Although some individual differences are bound to occur, sound basic skills relate to ultimate success in fencing. Various positions and movements have been developed and modified over hundreds of years, so that each position and each action serves a definite purpose. While fencing movements are not difficult, they can become automatic only by continual repetition. Practicing in front of a capable critic or a mirror is a good way to begin.

At first you will find that the foil feels awkward and unwieldly, but as you become accustomed to its feel it will become a part of you as you fence. Your movements will tend to be too large at first, but with practice they will become more controlled.

The Foil

Foil blades come in sizes from one to five, size one being the shortest. Children should use shorter blades, which are lighter and result in better control.

Adult preference has usually been for the longest, size five blade, but many fencers now use a number four. Electric blades are somewhat heavier and more point-heavy than nonelectric blades. The four blade provides better balance and control, particularly for an average to small person.

There is often a tendency for those with shorter arms to want the longest possible blade in order to extend their reach one more inch. However, this one extra inch comes at a relatively great loss in precision, and I do not recommend this costly compensation.

Directions in this book are geared mostly to the French handle. I believe it is the best because it has better balance than pistol grips due to the longer handle with

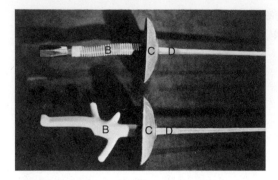

Figure 3.1
Foils. Top is a French foil and below is a pistol
grip foil. Pommel (A); handle (B); bell guard (C);
blade (D).

its counterbalancing pommel. In reality the French foil is heavier, but it doesn't feel
so point-heavy. The beauty of this weapon is that it is easier to develop the small,
precise movements so vital to good fencing. It is a more subtle weapon, relying on
speed rather than sheer force for effectiveness. It is also more effective for infighting, a tactic that will be discussed later.

Pistol (orthopedic) grips are shorter and lighter, making the blade more point-
heavy. Pistol grips are easier to learn to use on a beginning level, but the tendency
is to grip them more tightly. They do provide more strength for actions against an
opponent's blade. However, this frequently results in the fencer relying on strength
more than accuracy, thereby losing much of the essence of fine fencing, and con-
tributing to early fatigue.

A beginning fencer can get a false sense of security from the feeling of power
and the relative comfort of the pistol grip. The novice may have many victories
against other novices with this grip, but unless a relaxed grip is learned at a later
date, progress is sure to be very limited.

Once a fencer learns to control the French foil properly with a relatively light
grip, it is possible to switch to almost any other type of handle and use it effectively. I consider the French foil to be more versatile and a much better training
weapon than any other.

How to Hold the Foil

The rectangular French handle is not straight. The right-handed foil should be held
so that, with the wider sides on the top and bottom, the handle will curve upward
and to the right near the guard.

With the handle in this position, place the last joint of the thumb on top, about
one-half inch from the guard. Place the second joint of the forefinger on the bottom
so that it opposes the thumb. It is with these fingers that you will guide the foil.
Now rotate the hand so the knuckle of the thumb is at two o'clock. The remaining
three fingertips should rest on the left side of the handle where they will add
strength to the grip.

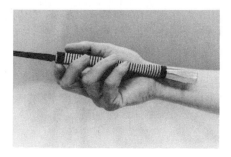

Figure 3.2
How to hold the French foil. (Photo by Robert Stadd)

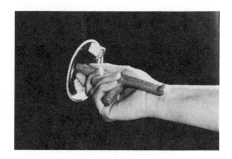

Figure 3.3
How to hold the pistol grip foil. The socket at the top of the guard is where the body cord plugs into the foil. (Photo by David Cary)

The foil must be gripped lightly yet firmly because a heavy or tense grip will result in large motions and will cause undue fatigue. The ability to manipulate the point with the smallest, quickest possible motions will depend on this relaxed but firm grip while the fingers guide the point. When you beat your opponent's blade or defend yourself, you will find that your fingers must tense to provide additional force, but they must relax when your blade is once more free.

The pommel lies against the center of the wrist so that the foil becomes an extension of the arm with no up or down break at the wrist. The palm of your hand should not touch the handle; instead there should be room in the palm of your hand for an imaginary mouse to be comfortably held beside the handle.

The pistol handle should be held and used similarly to the French handle with slight variations to adapt to the different handle shape. Two fingers go between the guard and first prong with the other two fingers resting on the second prong. The thumb rests on top as with the French handle. Too often beginning fencers grip this handle too tightly, resulting in fatigue and large actions. Hold the grip with the fingertips and leave room for the imaginary mouse to rest without being crushed. (*All directions that follow will be for the right-handed fencer. Left-handed fencers should reverse these directions.*)

Evaluation Question

What common error in gripping the foil causes fatigue and large, imprecise movements of the foil tip?

The On-Guard Position

The Salute

The salute, in one form or another, is as old as fencing itself, and has always been an unwritten requirement. As of 1994, however, fencing rules require fencers to salute not only your opponent, but also the referee and the audience, before and after a bout, and fencers will be penalized for failure to do so.

Figure 3.4
First position of the salute. (Photo by David Cary)

Figure 3.5
Second position of the salute. (Photo by David Cary)

Figure 3.6
Third position of the salute. (Photo by David Cary)

Whether taking a lesson, informally bouting, or competing in a tournament, whenever you cross blades, you must first salute, so the salute may be considered a standard preliminary to the on-guard position that is the basic fencing stance.

To begin the salute, fencers face each other, foil in hand, with the mask held under the left arm by the back piece, or tongue. The feet should be at right angles, with the right heel directly in front of the left heel and the right foot pointing in the direction of the other fencer. The left foot points to the side.

The salute is made in three quick, smooth motions. On count one, the foil arm is extended toward the floor; on count two, the foil comes up so that the guard almost touches the chin, point up; and on count three, the sword arm is extended shoulder high, with the point aiming at your opponent. After this quick salute, the mask is put on with the left hand, which is already holding it. The proper way to put the mask on is to put the chin in first so it rests on the chin pad, then pull the mask up and back over the top of the head in one quick motion. This method of putting on the mask not only looks nice but wastes very little time and tends to pull the hair back away from the face, which is important to those who have hair long enough to hang in their eyes.

The Leg Position

Now you are ready to assume the guard position in one motion. This stance will be broken down into its various parts so it can be learned bit by bit, but once you have become familiar with this position, it should be assumed quickly after the salute.

Figure 3.7
Front view of the on-guard position with the left hand clearly visible. Photographic angle makes the point seem higher than it is. (Photo by David Cary)

Figure 3.8
Side view of the on-guard position. (Photo by John Kedroff)

The feet remain at right angles with the right heel directly in front of the back one, but in the guard position the forward foot is moved ahead so that there is about a shoulder-width distance between the heels. Both knees bend so that they are over the toes with the body in the center, weight evenly distributed over the balls of the feet. In assuming this bent-knee position, be careful that only the legs move as the body is lowered. The body must not lean forward or backward; the pelvis should be directly under the trunk with shoulders and hips level.

The Arm Position

To bring the arms into position, carry the left arm behind the head. It should be bent at right angles, with the elbow at or just below shoulder height, the hand relaxed and hanging forward at about head level. In this position the left arm provides balance, helps keep the body in proper alignment, and is out of the way so it will not be hit. If kept in proper position, it will also add impetus to the attack and act somewhat like a rudder, as will be seen later in the discussion of the lunge.

When on guard, your left hand should be visible to your opponent. If the trailing hand is hidden you have turned your body too far to the side resulting in an unnatural, strained position. Ask a partner to check for visibility of the left hand, or face yourself in a mirror in the guard position and make sure you can see the left hand. Currently there is an unfortunate trend to let the rear arm lazily hang down, or low and to the side, but such a position eliminates the benefits in aiming and balance that the classic arm position offers.

The right, or sword, arm is bent so that the elbow is about eight inches in front of the body, with the hand held at chest level and the point at the height of the opponent's chin. You are now in the on-guard position.

In the on-guard position your body should be quite stable with no tendency to fall forward or backward, for you have lowered your center of gravity by bending your knees; the wide stance gives you a firm base of support with your body balanced in the center, hips under the trunk.

The sideways stance puts the sword in front where you will be in position to get maximum reach in the attack and where the arm will help to protect you since the right elbow should be in front of your body. This position also narrows the target, but it is a mistake to take an extreme sideways position in order to further minimize the target. If you find you have difficulty keeping the front foot and knee straight, turn the torso from the pelvis up to face slightly forward so that the leading knee and foot are in a natural position. An extreme sideways stance will restrict your attacking distance and will tend to cause your forward foot and knee to turn inward. While such a stance offers a minimum target, it also partially exposes your back, a valid target that is not as easily defended as the front of the target, making this not only an uncomfortable but an impractical position.

Evaluation Question

In assuming the on-guard position, is it more important to minimize the size of the target or to achieve a stable position, and why?

Footwork

The sport of fencing is only remotely related to the swashbuckling style of swordplay seen in the motion pictures, in which actors turn in circles, leap over tables, and swing from chandeliers. The surface on which you fence is called a *strip* (piste). The foil strip is from 1.5 to 2 meters (5 ft. to 6 ft. 7 in.) wide and 14 meters (46 ft.) long. Fencers are free to move back and forth as long as they remain on the strip without reversing positions. Fencers are often quite mobile on the strip, and excellent endurance is required to fence for any length of time due to the speed of the fencers' footwork as they move up and down the strip, each trying to draw the other a little too close, keeping on the move so that the other cannot have a chance to get set to attack at leisure, and each trying to get the other a little off balance so a swift attack can be successfully launched.

Advance

The advance brings you closer to your opponent. It is made by moving the forward foot ahead first about one shoe length with a heel-toe, walking step, then advancing the back foot the same distance. It is best to take short steps as you advance so you do not accidentally step into an attack or get too close to your opponent.

The advance is made in order to get close enough to attack if the opponent is out of distance. It also may be used to maintain a constant distance if the opponent has retreated or to force the opponent to retreat.

The advance should be a fast, smooth, gliding motion. There should be no bobbing of the head, no jerky leaping motions, and no dragging of the feet that will slow the footwork. The weight is carried on the balls of the feet, and the back foot provides speed by pushing you forward as you advance.

Retreat

The retreat is the reverse of the advance. It is done by first moving the left foot and then the right foot back about one shoe length. The feet should be the same distance apart at the end of the advance or retreat as they were originally.

The retreat may be used to make the opponent advance or to take you out of attacking distance as you defend against an attack. The retreat should also be made with a gliding motion.

Practicing the Advance and Retreat

From a proper on guard, try advancing several times while watching the tip of your foil, which will not bob up and down if you are moving smoothly. Next, practice retreating in the same manner. Finally, advance a few times, then retreat and so on until you are satisfied that your movements are smooth, quick, and controlled. As you move forward or backward, be sure that your feet never get closer together than they were when you began this exercise.

Lunge

The lunge is the extension of the guard position and is done in order to score against your opponent. It is the basic attacking position that brings you close enough to touch and in position for a quick recovery to the guard position at your regular fencing distance.

Evaluation Question

What are the purposes of the advance, and what effect do you think would result from bobbing your head as you move?

How to Lunge

All movements of the arm or blade must start with the point, which is guided into the desired position by the thumb and forefinger. The lunge also must start with the point, which is aimed at the exact spot you hope to hit or touch by pushing down on the handle with the thumb. Once the point is in line, the arm should be quickly and smoothly extended from the shoulder, with the hand slightly higher than the point. The shoulder must not be tensed or lifted because this will shorten your reach by at least an inch and cause your point to jump, spoiling your aim. Reach, rather than push, the blade forward.

This smooth, fast extension should be practiced until it becomes natural and easy, before the lunge itself is practiced.

Once the arm is working well, go on to the footwork of the lunge. Aim, extend the arm, then reach forward with the right foot and at the same time drive your body forward with the back foot, which remains flat on the floor during the lunge in order to maintain stability. The main force of the lunge is provided by the powerful extension of the left leg, which drives you forward. The left leg works much like a strong spring that is compressed as you crouch in the guard position, and hurls you forward as the spring, your leg, is released. The driving force that propels you forward must push straight forward through the hips, never up and forward.

At the same time the left leg extends, the left arm is flung down and back, palm up, so that it is in line with, and parallel to, the left leg. This backward extension of the arm helps provide force to the lunge and is a vital part of the lunge, for it quickly displaces your body weight forward. If the left arm moves sideways when you lunge, you will find that you easily can lose your balance and your aim.

At the end of the lunge, your body should be in the following position: the right knee bent directly over the right instep, not over or in front of the toe because this will put undue strain on the knee and thigh slowing your recovery; hips still under the trunk, facing almost forward; trunk straight but leaning a little toward the point; shoulders level, both arms and left leg straight; and left foot flat on the floor (see fig. 3.9).

Recovery from the lunge is made by pushing from the right heel while pulling the body back with the recoiling rear leg. At the same time, return both arms to a bent guard position. Be sure to bend the left leg when you recover so that you will be in your beginning stance, never standing upright. It takes much less energy to return to a crouch position than to a standing one, and only in this lower position are you ready to continue fencing, which may be necessary if your attack did not land.

Practicing the Lunge

At first the lunge should be practiced slowly and analyzed at each step until you are sure you understand how to lunge correctly. Be sure that the extension of the foil

Figure 3.9
The lunge. (Photo by David Cary)

Figure 3.10
The lunge. (Photo by David Cary)

arm always precedes the advancement of the forward foot. Imagine there is a string attached to the foil hand and to the front toes. As your arm reaches its full extension, the imaginary string will lift your foot to begin the lunge. As you practice remember that the extended arm pulls the foot forward.

The beginning fencer often feels that the arm extension will telegraph the intent to attack to the opponent, but this is not so. For one thing, there are many times you may extend your foil arm without making an attack. Another factor difficult to realize at first is that in an attack that begins with a bent arm (that is, when the foot moves before the arm) the moving front shoulder is much more visible than a smoothly reaching arm.

You will need to stretch gradually until you are able to perform a full, deep lunge without feeling any strain. As soon as you feel sure of the various elements of the lunge you should begin working for speed and force, which can be acquired only through continual repetition. Many top-ranking fencers lunge at least one hundred times daily to keep themselves flexible and forceful in their attacks.

Common Errors

1. Failing to extend the foil arm before moving the leading foot. This telegraphs your attack and fails to establish right-of-way. Always lead with the point of the foil.
2. Taking too long a step when you lunge. If you overlunge, it is very difficult to recover to the guard position. Be sure your knee is over the instep of your leading foot.
3. Taking too short a step when you lunge. If you take a short step and then try to lean forward to reach a target, you put a strain on your front knee and limit your reach. Step as far as you need to reach, but never let the forward knee end up in front of your leading foot.
4. Dropping the forward shoulder and hip when you lunge. This opens your shoulder, which is a valid target, and shortens your reach considerably. Keep the shoulders and hips level with the floor.
5. Rolling over the back foot onto the ankle. This puts a strain on the back knee and decreases body stability. Keep the back foot firmly on the floor.
6. Failing to lower the back arm, or lowering the back arm after lunging. This will lessen the force of your lunge. The back arm should provide part of the forward impetus for the lunge.

Fencers today rarely remain static on the strip. You will need to be able to cover ground quickly, either forward or backward; therefore the advance, retreat, and lunge should be practiced until they become natural movements for you. Then try various combinations of these actions.

Advance-Lunge

It often is necessary to attack with an advance-lunge since much fencing today is done out of distance, so a lunge will not reach the opponent. This is a safer distance for fencing since it gives more time for the defense, but it does require the ability to cover this distance, often with great speed.

Fencing distance is lunging distance from an opponent. If an opponent fences within fencing distance but habitually retreats as you attack, the advance-lunge will enable you to gain extra distance so the lunge can bring you near enough for the attack to succeed. It is essential that you keep all parts of your body under control throughout any actions you make. If you overlunge or lose your balance in any way, it may be relatively easy for your opponent to score; so while all-out speed and determination are required in the attack, your body must also be controlled by keeping your left foot firmly on the floor during the lunge and by balancing correctly.

In a simple advance-attack, the sword arm must be extended at the start of the advance, since this is the beginning of the attack, and it must remain extended throughout the attack. Any time the arm is withdrawn during an attack, the attacker loses right-of-way and may be hit by a quick thrust from the other fencer. To make this advance-attack, you should first extend your arm as you start to advance, then lunge with no hesitation between movements.

Evaluation Question

If your lunge fails to touch a retreating opponent, may you legally continue your attack and, if so, how?

Lunge, Recover Forward, Lunge

If your opponent has retreated just out of reach as you lunge, you may recover forward from the lunge by bending the left leg and bringing it forward to put you in the guard position. From this position you can defend or advance to a better position.

You may also recover forward and immediately lunge again, thus continuing the attack against an opponent who has momentarily relaxed, confident in a mistaken sense of security. To continue such an attack from the lunge, the back foot should recover to a distance just short of the usual guard position. With the foot well behind your hips and your weight just a little forward, it is possible to make a smooth, strong lunge to catch the unsuspecting opponent. Care must be taken to keep the body position low during this "reprise" of the attack.

Fencing Distance

Fencing distance, or the distance between two fencers, depends on the length of the lunge. Fencers should be far enough apart so that a full lunge can just reach the opponent. You should never be on guard closer than this distance or you will be too easily scored upon, but you may fence farther apart if you desire. It is important that you quickly become accustomed to your lunging distance so that you will not make the mistake of fencing too closely, a mistake common to beginners. If one fencer has a longer lunge than the other, you should fence at the distance of the longer reach.

To learn your lunging distance you can practice by placing the tip of your foil against a wall, lunging pad, or partner, and extending your arm as you assume a guard position so that, with your arm extended, the foil reaches the target with a slight bend in the blade. From this position, reach backward with the back leg until you are lowered into a full lunge. Now, without moving the back foot, recover backward to your guard position, which will put you at your lunging distance from the target. Lunge several times, being careful not to allow the back foot to creep forward. Be aware of the distance as you learn just how far you can reach with a full lunge.

Practice Drills

Find your lunging distance from a partner, preferably one of the same general height as yourself. Study this distance until you feel familiar with it. Next, one of you should take the initiative in advancing or retreating, *one step at a time,* while the other fencer maintains a constant fencing distance by retreating as the partner advances or vice versa. The object of this exercise is to learn to adjust your distance quickly and evenly with proper footwork. Be careful to maintain your body weight evenly between your feet, rather than shift it from foot to foot as you move.

Common Errors

1. Moving the wrong foot first in an advance or a retreat. Always move the front foot first to advance and the back foot first to retreat.
2. Moving one foot farther than the other during the advance or retreat. Each must move the same distance.
3. Shifting your body weight over one foot or the other as you move. Keep your weight balanced between your feet at all times.
4. Taking large steps as you move. Several small steps are better than a few long ones.

Practice lunging several times, making sure your body alignment and balance are good. Then practice any combination of advance-lunge; lunge-recover forward-lunge; retreat-advance-lunge; lunge-recover-retreat; and so on.

Engagement

Contact of the feebles of the blades for protection while in the guard position is called *engagement* of the blades. When fencers are lunging distance apart, they may engage blades. If your opponent's blade is to the left of yours, move your blade left so that a simple lunge could not land against you, and if the blade is to the right of yours, move your blade right to protect that line. If two right-handers or two left-handers are working together, they will both be engaged in the same line.

Figure 3.11
Engagement of blades, in fencing distance.
(Photo by David Cary)

In the engagement, contact should be made lightly with no pushing of the blades. With this light contact, your fingers are sensitive enough to feel the slightest movement made by your opponent's hand even before you can see the motion.

Fingering

Fingering refers to the manipulation of the foil tip by the action of the thumb and forefinger. It is essential for a fencer to be able to move the point in this manner so that there will be no superfluous motion that is time consuming or motion that enables the opponent to see what you are doing.

Change of Engagement

Change of engagement is made by passing the point of the foil under the feeble of the opponent's blade to engage it on the opposite side. The point must move the smallest distance with very delicate fingering. The point should move first to contact the other side of the blade, and then the hand moves to the new guard position.

The change is useful in maintaining control over your opponent's foil. If, for instance, you feel that the other fencer is about to attack, a quick change of engagement may upset those plans. You may change engagement in order to get control of the other blade prior to attacking or when advancing to maintain blade contact and lessen chances of a surprise attack that may be initiated against you when you advance.

Double Change of Engagement

Double change of engagement consists of two rapid changes of engagement without moving the hand. A proficient fencer often attacks as an opponent advances, because for a brief instant one cannot retreat out of distance. A quick double change as you advance makes it very difficult for the other person to attack. The double change can be used in the same way as a single change. These actions should both be used, but not continually. Remember that you must always keep the opponent guessing as to what you will do next, so you must be careful to avoid doing any one thing repeatedly.

The double change is good fingering practice because it strengthens the fingers. It also requires a relaxed grip; therefore, it can serve as a reminder to keep your hand and arm loose as you fence.

Practice Drills

Working with a partner, change engagement several times while one fencer holds a steady guard position. Next, practice the double change of engagement in the same manner, and then reverse roles. Repeat this drill, but advance just after the point moves to change or double change. Your opponent should retreat as you advance to maintain correct fencing distance. Work for speed, finesse, and ability to control an opponent's blade without trying to push or move it.

Absence of the Blade

You may also fence without engaging the other blade. This is called *absence of the blade*. Although you lack the feel and control of your opponent's blade in this instance, you will, by the same token, not have your blade controlled by the other person. This type of fencing requires good distance and visual alertness at all times.

Evaluation Question

What are the advantages and disadvantages when you fence without engaging the opponent's blade?

Lines

The target is theoretically divided into four lines, or sections: high inside (4), high outside (6), low inside (7), and low outside (8). The upper lines are above the foil hand, and the lower lines are below it. The inside lines are toward the front of the body, or to the left of the sword hand for right-handers; and the outside lines are toward the back, or to the right of the sword hand (see fig. 3.12). The hand moves left or right as necessary to protect the target.

There are two guard positions for each line: one with the hand in supination, in which the palm faces up, and one in pronation, or palm down. The supination parries are the ones usually used in foil fencing, while the pronation parries are used in sabre. With the four supination positions you can readily protect any area of the target.

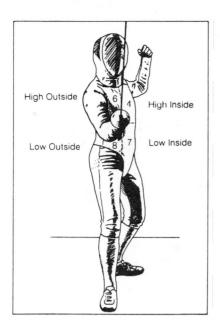

High Outside

High Inside

Low Outside

Low Inside

Figure 3.12
The lines of 4, 6, 7, and 8.

Defense

Parries

The defense with the blade is called a *parry*. This may be either a blocking parry, which is made by moving the sword to protect yourself by blocking the attack, or a beat parry, which is made by spanking the opponent's blade sharply. The blocking parry is more useful against a powerful attack, against a fencer who is too close, or against one who tries to hit by jabbing repeatedly. The beat parry is more useful against a clean attack because it frees your blade so that you may immediately score after your defense.

Either type of parry is made by moving the point and hand to the desired line, so that you may parry in four, six, seven, or eight (see figs. 3.13–3.20). There must be no backswing and no follow-through, either of which would momentarily expose your target and consume additional time. The flexible tip of the blade whips laterally at any sharp impact, but it will quickly right itself if the hand is kept under careful control. Any large motions will result in still more point deviation, making it very difficult to guide the point accurately. You must try to stop the point just over the edge of your opponent's shoulder in the high lines, or beside the knee in

High Inside

Figure 3.13
Parry of four. (Photo by Ric Thompson) .

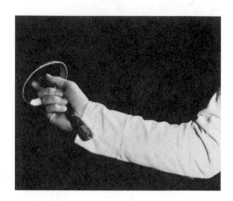

Figure 3.14
Hand position for the guard of four. (Photo by David Cary)

High Outside

Figure 3.15
Parry of six. (Photo by Ric Thompson)

Figure 3.16
Hand position for the guard of six. (Photo by David Cary)

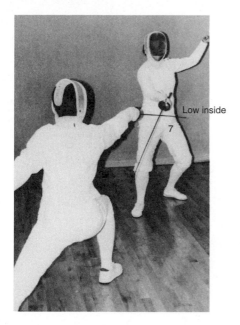

Figure 3.17
Parry of seven. (Photo by Ric Thompson)

Figure 3.18
Hand position for the guard or parry of seven. (Photo by David Cary)

the low lines. From the proper parry positions, you only need to aim the point and quickly extend to score after a successful defense. The actions of attacking after a parry is called a *riposte*.

Parry Four

The high-inside line is that of four (*quarte*). The hand moves to the left until it is in front of the left side of your body, point over the edge of your opponent's right shoulder. In this position, the wrist breaks laterally so the pommel is not against the wrist, but the handle remains under the base of the thumb. The thumb knuckle is at one o'clock.

Parry Six

The high-outside line is six (*sixte*). The hand moves to the right so that it is in front of the right side of your body, point over the opponent's left shoulder. This tends to be a weaker position than four for many people, much as the backhand stroke in tennis is often weaker than the forehand. In order to assure a strong six position, rotate the hand slightly to the right so that the knuckle of the thumb is at two o'clock, and brace the pommel against the inside of the wrist for additional support. In this position there should be a straight line from the elbow through the foil.

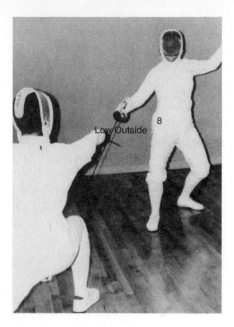

Low Outside 8

Figure 3.19
Parry of eight. (Photo by Ric Thompson)

Figure 3.20
Hand position for the guard or parry of eight. (Photo by David Cary)

Parry Seven

Seven (*septime*) defends the low-inside line. From the high lines of four or six, the move to seven is made by breaking the wrist downward as the point moves clockwise, stopping just beyond the opponent's knee. The hand is to the left of the body as it was in four, still at chest height with the palm of the hand facing up.

Parry Eight

The guard of eight (*octave*) defends the low-outside line. From four or six, the blade moves counterclockwise, aiming at the inside of the opponent's knee. The hand pivots to the new position as the wrist breaks down, palm of the hand up. The forearm does not drop.

When a parry is made, the sword arm should neither extend nor bend from the guard position unless the opponent is closer than the normal fencing distance, in which case the arm will have to be withdrawn in order to parry. All parries should deflect the opponent's blade to the side, never up or down, for this may result in an invalid touch to the legs or head. The target is longer than it is wide, so the most effective parry is lateral.

When parrying, always meet your opponent's blade with a corner of your blade rather than with its flat side; the smaller surface of an edge can deliver more force for a beat or parry. Proper hand position will assure such a blade position. Parry with the center or forte of the blade.

Evaluation Question

Where should you try to stop the blade point in the high lines and in the low lines? What advantage does your opponent gain if your movement is too large?

Types of Parries

Direct Parries

These are made by moving the sword to the left or right to defend either the high or low lines. If a fencer is on guard in six, the line of four will be open, so an attack to the line of four may be defended by the direct parry of four.

Semicircular Parries

Semicircular parries occur when moving from high to low or from low to high lines, since the tip of the blade describes an arc as it crosses the body to remove the threatening blade laterally.

Circular, or Counter-Parries

These are made by changing lines with a small, circular motion of the blade. Circular parries may seem to be slow, but they can be made very quickly because the hand need not change lines and the parry is made with the thumb, forefinger, and wrist as the point is guided under the attacking blade and returned to the original position with a quick, small, powerful action. For instance, if a fencer is on guard in four, the high-outside line of six will be unprotected, so an attack to this open line may be parried with a parry of counter four. The foil hand is in the position of four and remains in four during the parry. Similarly, a fencer whose hand is in the sixth position may defend against an attack to the fourth line with a parry of counter six.

It is important for a fencer to be able to make either a direct or circular parry in any line and to vary the use of them. You will find that any time an opponent can accurately predict what you will do—that is, how you will attack or parry—you are vulnerable, so outwitting your opponent is a major part of fencing. Changing your defense is one way of keeping the other person guessing, thereby making it more difficult to plan an attack.

Practice Drills

Take a guard position in six with your body parallel to a wall, rear toe and knee touching the wall. Quickly move to parry in four. Do not crash into the wall, but stop with the guard and point just touching the wall. Repeat, moving from seven to eight. Next, turn your back to the wall, front foot and back heel about three inches from the wall, and similarly parry from four to six, and from seven to eight.

Engage blades with a partner, making sure that you are the correct fencing distance apart. Begin with the guard of four so that you both guard the upper-inside line of four with your partner's blade to the left of yours. (If one partner is

Figure 3.21
Direct parry as it moves from six to parry in four. (Photo by David Cary)

Figure 3.22
Semicircular parry as it moves from six to parry in eight. (Photo by David Cary)

Figure 3.23
Circular (counter) parry as it starts from six and returns to six, picking up the attacker's blade. (Photo by David Cary)

left-handed, that hand will be in six.) Beat the other blade without moving your arm, then allow the partner to beat your blade. Take turns beating in four, being careful to maintain point control. Beat with the middle third of the blade.

One partner may change engagement to six and repeat the drill in that line, then similarly beat in the lines of seven and eight. As a progression, one partner may lunge to the fourth line as the other fencer defends in four. Take turns attacking this way in each of the four lines.

Common Errors in Defense

1. Taking a backswing, which results in too large an action.
2. Parrying further than necessary, thereby exposing the target rather than covering it.
3. Parrying with a windshield-wiper action so that the parry beats the attacking blade down rather than sideways. Think of the blade as a wall that moves laterally to protect a line.
4. Bending or extending the arm when parrying. Unless your opponent is very close, your arm should not withdraw to parry.

Evaluation Question

When you parry, should you meet the opponent's blade with the flat side or a corner of your blade and why? Should the contact be made near the tip of your blade or at its center?

Figure 3.24
Thrust to low line of eight with the hand in pronation. (Photo by David Cary)

Figure 3.25
Right-hand thrust to left-hander's line of four, hand in pronation. Left-hander would thrust similarly to right-hander.

Attacks

Touching the Opponent

Before actually attacking another person, it is important to learn to make a soft touch as opposed to a hard, or jabbing, touch.

The action that touches the opponent is called a *thrust*. It is advisable to first thrust at a wall target by taking the guard position just far enough away so that, by extending your arm, you reach the target firmly enough to cause the blade to bend slightly upward. Once the feeling of thrusting with the arm is acquired, the same thing should be tried from the full lunging distance. The thrust should be firm and quick, but not hard.

When you are thrusting well with a full lunge, do the same thing against another person. As soon as possible, you must develop the feel of placing the point on the target with the fingers, and you must learn to be touched without flinching. A good way to practice at first is for partners to get on-guard, lunging distance apart, and to take turns lunging and touching each other without attempting to defend themselves. Later the defense may be added as attacks increase in speed and skill.

In most instances the thrust should be made with the hand in the sixth position, palm up with the thumb knuckle at two o'clock. In this position the point will dip slightly toward the target. Remember that the arm and hand must be shoulder high if your target is a high line.

There are times when it is wiser to thrust with your hand in a pronated, or palm down, position. Any time a right-handed person attacks the low-outside line of eight with the palm up, the blade will bend away from the target and slide past rather than making a clean touch. By turning your hand, palm down, you will find your point again bending toward your target.

Figure 3.26
Right-handed thrust to left-hander's line of eight. Hand is in supination. Left-handers would hit a right-hander in the same way.

Left-Handed Modification

Left-handed fencers are often frustrated to find that well executed attacks regularly slide past their right-handed target. This is generally because the blade naturally bends away from the target when the hand is in the sixth position. In order to get a clean touch against a fencer who is opposite-handed, turn your hand slightly so that the point bends into the target (see fig. 3.25).

With a partner (right-hander against left-hander), extend your sword arm toward either high line and slightly rotate your hand until you find the position at which your point will aim into the target. Learn to keep your hand positioned in this manner when attacking.

The above applies equally to right-handed fencers working with left-handers.

Simple Attacks

Simple attacks are those consisting of just one quick action. These attacks rely on speed, proper distance, and surprise, or timing. There are three simple attacks.

Straight Thrust

This is usually a fast lunge with no change of line during the attack. It is occasionally a very good attack but cannot be used often against a good fencer.

The straight thrust can be used against an opponent who is not protected in the guard position. Fencers often fence with "absence of the blade" while on guard, leaving the line to which the opponent's blade points unprotected. This is most common when fencing out of distance or more than lunging distance apart. If you can maneuver such a fencer to within fencing distance, it may be possible to score with an explosive straight thrust.

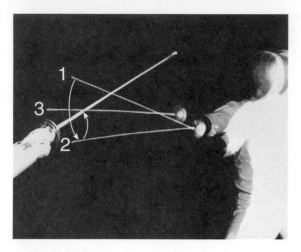

Figure 3.27
Disengage attack. 1. Blades engaged in four; 2. point passes under the defender's blade as the arm extends; 3. point is aimed and the fencer lunges to score in six. (Photo by John Kedroff)

Disengage

When the line in which you are engaged is closed (protected), you may change lines to score with a disengage. This movement is made by guiding the point under the opponent's blade with the fingers making the smallest motion needed to clear the blade, then reaching and lunging. It should be made as one continuous motion. The blade stays close to the opponent's blade so that the action will be fast and difficult to see.

The tip of the blade should describe a **V** in this attack. First, the fingers drop the point to the lower point of the **V** without moving the arm and then aim to the top of the **V** while extending the arm, and finally, the fencer lunges. This is one continuous, smooth motion. You may disengage from any line to any other unprotected line, low or high, but when changing from seven to eight, or from eight to seven, the disengage will be made over the blade rather than under it.

The disengage is easy to do if blades are engaged in any line. However, because fencers often fence with "absence of the blade," they may both be in eight or six, but with blades not touching. In this case, a disengage would only take you into a closed line, an obvious waste of time. Do not give up too easily on the disengage because it is still one of the most useful attacks you can make. This attack can be effectively made when your opponent attempts to contact your blade, either to beat or to engage your blade, but it requires alertness and fine timing to attack without letting your opponent actually find your blade.

Cutover (Coupé)

The cutover is similar to the disengage in that it involves a change of line. However, instead of dropping under the blade you lift over it. To make a cutover, lift your point over the opponent's point with your fingers. As your point clears to the

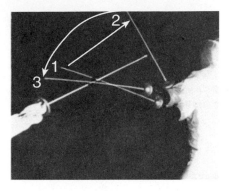

Figure 3.28
Cutover (coupé). 1. Blades engaged in four; 2. point lifts over the defender's blade; 3. point aims and the arm extends to score in six. (Photo by John Kedroff)

new line, forcefully aim, again with the action of your fingers, fixing your point to the intended target. As your point aims, extend your arm and lunge so that the described action flows in a continuous, smooth motion.

Common Faults

1. Lunging before the point is aimed, causing the arm to withdraw during the attack. Begin the attack with the point.
2. Bending the elbow and lifting the point too high to clear the tip of the other blade. The cutover should be made with the fingers, not the arm.
3. Failing to fix to point to the intended target.

Compound Attacks

Any attack made up of two or more actions is a compound attack. In a compound attack, one or more preparatory actions are followed by the final, or thrusting, part of the attack. In any such attack, the attacker gains right-of-way by extending the arm but may lose it on bending the arm during the attack, so in these attacks the arm must be extended to gain right-of-way. An advance is not an attack, nor is a lunge in which the arm does not extend considered an attack.

Preparatory Actions

Feint

The feint is intended to look like an attack. Its purpose is to cause a reaction that will open the line to which the real attack will be made. It is made by aiming and extending the foil arm to menace any open line. A static extension will probably not fool any but the very nervous fencer. To make the feint seem convincing it may be helpful to shift your weight a little by reaching forward from your waist. It should be a strong, decisive action.

Figure 3.29
Feint. The arm extends, point in line.

You can feint a straight thrust, feint a disengage, or feint a cutover. It is important to make this feint visible in order to draw a proper response.

Common Faults

1. Making a quick feint, then withdrawing your arm. Such an action will never draw the desired reaction. Hold the arm extension long enough to get results.
2. Failing to aim to a definite spot. Merely waving the point around will not accomplish anything. Be sure to strongly aim to a specific point.

Beat

This is similar to a beat-parry except that, as an offensive action, the beat is made with the middle third of the blade. It is made with a clean, sharp, spanking motion to either side of the blade. The beat may be very strong to open the line to be hit, or it may be a light beat to cause an answering beat from your opponent, thereby opening the opposite line for a disengage or cutover attack.

Common Faults

1. Taking a backswing before the beat. Beat with the fingers.
2. Bending the arm with the beat. This will increase the distance you must travel to score.
3. Allowing your point to wander after the beat. Fix your point after beating so your second action will be properly controlled.

Press

The press is similar to the beat but is a more subtle action. The fingers grip the handle forcefully to push, or press, the other blade. There should be no arm or hand motion, and the point must not move out of line but must be kept under control for the action that is to follow. Usually this is done to cause the opponent to press in return, and may be followed by a disengage or cutover.

Glide

This motion consists of gliding the blade along that of the opponent as the arm extends. It is similar to the feint and is useful against a light hand.

Derobement (Deceiving a Beat)

As the opponent attempts to beat your blade, perhaps in answer to a beat, you may attack by dropping your point just low enough for the beat to pass over your blade without hitting it, then attack with a disengage. If you began in the line of six, you will end in the line of four, even though you did not move your blade to the side very much as your opponent made the lateral movement for you. This is a little like jump rope in that you avoid being hit by the jump rope by going under it.

You may also deceive a circular (counter) beat in the same manner to make a counter disengage attack.

Some Examples of Compound Attacks

By combining one or more preparatory actions before the final thrust, you can make a wide variety of compound attacks.

One-Two. Feint a disengage to an unprotected line. If your opponent attempts a direct parry, deceive the parry with a disengage and lunge to score.

Doublé. Feint a disengage, just as for the one-two, but if a counter parry instead of a direct parry is made against the feint, deceive the counter parry by making a circle around the parry. In this attack there is no change of direction as the point disengages, then continues in the same direction until it completes a full circle and one-half to land in the line first threatened by the feint. This may be described as a corkscrew attack.

Feint a Straight Thrust, Disengage, or Counter Disengage. Much of the time fencers prefer the guard of six with no blade contact. When this is so, a simple feint without changing line may force a parry that can be avoided with a disengage if the parry is direct.

If the feint is met with a counter parry, the counter disengage should be used. This action circles around the parrying blade just as in the double described above. The difference between a counter disengage and a double is that in the counter disengage the feint does not change lines. That is, feint a straight thrust, disengage, avoiding a counter parry. Too often a fencer decides on a particular attack because it is a favorite, rather than because it is the correct attack. If this sounds repetitious, it is because it deserves repeating. **Plan attacks around your opponent's defense.**

Defense against Feint Attacks. When an attacker successfully deceives your parry of his or her feint, you must make a second parry. You can, for instance, try to parry a feint to the high-inside line with a parry of four, then parry a deceiving disengage with either a parry of counter four or direct six. It is a mistake to parry too quickly because this aids an attacker who wishes to make a one-two or double attack. It is better to wait until the attacker is fairly deep to parry.

Other Compound Attacks. There are numerous other compound attacks. For example, you can beat, or press, and straight thrust, disengage, or cutover; beat in the opposite line and straight thrust, cutover, or disengage; or feint any simple attack and disengage.

Attacks usually should not consist of more than two or three movements because an attack that takes too long to execute may be stopped before its completion by a counteraction from your opponent. Often the simplest attacks, made with great speed and accuracy at just the right time, are the most effective ones.

Hitting with Opposition

If fencers are engaged in four, their hands are to the left of their torsos. When one of them makes a disengage to six, the attacker's hand should change to the position of six as the arm extends in order to close off his or her own line of six as the attacking blade opposes the defender's blade, thereby protecting the attacker's target from the defender. Similarly, if fencers are engaged in six, when attacking to the line of four, the attacker's hand should change to the fourth position for protection.

You must be sure to make the line change before lunging so that there will be no tendency to withdraw the arm during the attack.

Common Faults

1. Lunging before aiming or extending the arm. Always lead with the point, not the foot.
2. Moving the arm and/or point in a wide **U** rather than a small **V.**
3. Withdrawing the arm during the change of line.

Attacks in Advance

When you fence out of distance, or when you feel certain that your opponent will retreat out of distance as you advance, you may advantageously make an advance-attack to get within scoring distance. The shorter fencer must master this particular kind of attack in order to compensate for a shorter lunging distance. Any compound attack of two or three actions can be made in advance effectively. The feint, beat, or press is made as you advance; the final thrust is made as you lunge. For example, the one-two attack in advance is made by feinting a disengage while advancing and then making the final disengage while lunging.

Practice Drills

Working with a partner, designate one fencer as the attacker. The attacker should feint a straight thrust and try to deceive a parry with a disengage lunge, making sure that there is no blade contact. If the defender finds the attacker's blade, the attack was not properly timed. After several successful attacks, the attacker should become the defender so that both fencers may practice. As the skill of each partner increases, the defender may parry with direct or counter parries, and the attacker may attempt to deceive them, but this is very difficult.

Later, the attacker may make an advance as the defender retreats and parries. Some attacks should be allowed to reach, and some should be parried by making a second parry. If a feint is correctly timed, there should not be any blade contact. If, on the other hand, the blade is clearly met by the defender during the feint, the attack has failed.

In a more advanced drill that is especially challenging, one fencer may make either feint attacks or simple attacks in a random pattern, while the other fencer tries to parry only attacks, never feints. This requires feints to be strong and convincing in order to draw the desired response, and helps defenders to control their responses to feints and attacks. The ideal would be to never parry a feint unless you are setting a trap for your opponent.

Common Faults

1. Lunging too soon. This causes the attacker's arm to withdraw during the attack, thereby losing right-of-way. Lunge when you are ready to score, not during your preparation.
2. Attacking from too far away. You must know you will reach your target.
3. Lack of confidence in an attack. If you doubt the success of an attack, there will be a tendency to withdraw the sword arm to parry before the attack is completed. Be sure of an attack or do not begin it. Confidence comes from repeated trials with full intent to score. Use attacks in practice until you can make them work.
4. Failure to feint convincingly. The feint must look like an attack, which means that you must extend your arm reach toward a threatened target rather than simply make a bent-arm feint to open air.
5. Overlunging, which causes a fencer to lose control and the ability to recover quickly to the guard position. Be sure of your distance before attacking, and never try to reach beyond the point of control.

Right-of-Way

Right-of-way has been briefly explained earlier in this chapter, but more needs to be said about this extremely important concept. When two fencers make a touch at the same time, one fencer usually has right-of-way. Occasionally two fencers attack and touch simultaneously, in which case no touch can be awarded, but this is more the exception than the rule. Even if one fencer makes a valid touch and the other an off-target hit, no touch will be awarded in such a case. The first consideration is to determine right-of-way.

Remember, right-of-way may be gained by extending the foil arm, point directed at the opponent's target. Right-of-way would be lost by this fencer if his or her blade is deflected or if the extended arm is withdrawn, if it is parried, or if the attack misses altogether. If a feint or attack is parried by the opponent, right-of-way passes to the defender who made the parry. The defender may then take advantage of this right-of-way by attacking without delay. Right-of-way is not a factor if two fencers attempt to score and only one actually touches the opponent. In that case the touch is awarded whether the scoring fencer had right-of-way or not.

Right-of-way rules favor an orderly exchange of actions. For example:

fencer A attacks fencer B;
fencer B defends and attacks fencer A (riposte);
fencer A defends and again attacks fencer B (counter riposte);
and so on until one fencer is touched, valid, or off target.

Riposte

As stated before, the riposte is an offensive action that is made by a fencer who has parried an attack. The riposte can be simple or compound and can be made to any line. It can be made with a lunge if the opponent recovers to the guard position quickly, or it can be made by thrusting without a lunge if it is made quickly enough to arrive before the opponent has had time to recover.

Fencers should practice the riposte after each successful defense so that it becomes a natural reaction after a parry. Be sure that the parry is complete before beginning the riposte. It is a mistake to start the riposte in anticipation of making a good parry because then the tendency is to extend the arm while you think "riposte" before actually making the parry. The proper sequence of action should be; attack, parry, aim, then riposte.

Remise

The remise is an attacker's second attempt to score when the original attempt fails. While still in the lunge, the attacker may attempt to place the point on the target. The remise does not have right-of-way over an immediate riposte.

Reprise

The reprise is a retaking of the attack. The attack may be resumed if an attack fails and there is no riposte. It is a new action as opposed to replacing the point as in the remise.

Redoublement

The redoublement is a retaking of the attack after regaining the guard position, either by recovering forward or backward, when there is no riposte.

Suggested Readings

Alaux, Michel. *Modern Fencing*. New York: Charles Scribner's and Sons, 1975.

Campos, Jules. *The Art of Fencing*. New York: Vantage Press, 1989.

Gillet, Jean-Jacques. *Foil Techniques & Terminology*. New Jersey: U.S. Academy of Arms, 1981.

Lukovich, István. *Fencing*. Hungary: Alföldi Printing House, Debrecen, 1986. Rev. John Harvie. Newbury Books, 1986.

Pitman, Brian. *Fencing Techniques of Foil, Epee, and Sabre*. U.K.: Crowood, 1989.

Shaff, Jo. *Fencing*. New York: Atheneum, 1982.

Simmonds, A. T., and Morton, E. D. *Start Fencing*. U.K.: Sportsmans Press, 1990.

Beginning to Bout

4

The desire to test your ability to use learned basic skills against another fencer is natural. Realize that reactions to unpredictable actions will be too large and first attempts to bout will result in imperfect form. Be patient and keep working on form, and you will improve both in control and in the ability to decide what actions will be appropriate in varying situations.

What You Must Know Before You Begin to Bout

In informal bouting practice there are certain conventions that should be observed. Fencers start equidistant from the center of the strip, far enough apart so that when on guard, with arms extended, foil tips will not touch.[1] Whether on a regulation fencing strip or a corner of a gym, each fencer should have the same retreat distance as you begin. Once you actually start to bout, continue fencing until a point lands or until fencing becomes sloppy and actions unclear. A fencer who is touched should acknowledge the touch by raising the back hand or saying "touch," or "off target," if the point landed anywhere but on the valid target.

When a valid touch is scored, fencers return to the center of the strip and proceed as before. A valid touch is one that lands on the torso with the tip of the foil. When an off-target touch is made, action stops immediately, blades are again crossed, and action resumes at the place where the foul occurred. Since an off-target hit stops action, a fencer who, for instance, touches the opponent's arm and then the valid target, does not score. Fencing does not stop when a point slaps or merely grazes the opponent because these actions are misses, not touches.

A bout is over when one fencer has scored five times. You should get to know the rules as you fence in order to increase your enjoyment of bouting. For an overview of fencing rules, see chapter 8.

When You Begin to Fence

Now for the actual bout. You will salute, put on your mask, and get on-guard in six. Now what? Realize that a fencing bout follows a regular sequence of actions. Either fencer may attack to take right-of-way. The defender may take right-of-way from the attacker by successfully parrying, at which time the defender may now turn attacker. The attack made by the defender is called a *riposte*. The logical chain of events then is attack, parry, riposte, parry, counter riposte, and so on until an action lands. If a defender parries but fails to riposte, the attacker may retake right-of-way and continue to attack.

Now you are ready to fence. Advance and retreat to see how well your opponent follows—if at all. As you move, does your opponent get a little too close? If so, why not attack very quickly to any *open line*. If your attack worked, fine, do it again. If it did not work, why did it fail? You may have been too slow or you may have telegraphed your attack by leading with your body or foot, rather than with your point, or perhaps your distance was wrong. It is important to keep at it until your attacks begin to work. Remember, surprise and speed are necessary for a simple attack to succeed.

Attack with conviction, even if you feel unsure at this point. This means that you must see where and how you will score before you begin an attack. Imagine you see and feel the point land, then do it. Often beginning fencers hesitate in an attack because they fear the opponent will counterattack or riposte during their attack. Know that your extended arm attack has the right-of-way unless it is parried, and be confident in your simple attack.

If your attack is parried, immediately withdraw your arm to a defensive position, preferably to four. Your arm can bend even though your body is lunging. Try to develop the reflex to withdraw your arm when you feel and hear steel find your blade during an attack, but not before.

Fencers must be ready to defend against an attack any time they are within scoring distance, so if you wish to relax for a moment and think, retreat and do so out of distance. When you are attacked, retreat a step and move to defend the threatened line with your blade when you are sure this is really an attack and not just a feint.

When your simple attack is parried, it is time to change your tactics. Try a feint-disengage attack that is calculated to deceive the parry your opponent will surely make again. Conversely, when your parry does not find steel because the attacker is using a feint-attack, be ready to parry a second time as you retreat in order to stop your opponent's compound attack.

Avoid the tendency to make one action and stop. If your attack is parried, redouble and try again if there is no riposte. If your opponent ripostes, defend and counter riposte. It is very hard to react properly to these various actions on the spot, but realize that your opponent will probably react in the same way at your next attack, particularly if you are working with another beginner. This allows you to plan your follow-up moves.

Always work to improve your technique as you fence. Know what attacks succeed and which ones fail. If they fail, ask yourself why? How can you make them work?

Beginning fencers often seem to continually beat blades, probably because they have seen many movie duels in which frequent beats are the rule, used to increase viewer interest. In reality, such beating is a useless tactic. Avoid any repetitive pattern unless you deliberately use it to set up the other fencer. Repetitive beating may set you up for a disengage attack from your opponent who can deceive your beats and attack.

Figure 4.1
The retreating fencer on the left has successfully defended against an attack before the lunge was completed. (Photo by David Cary)

Figure 4.2
An all-out attack is parried. (Photo by David Cary)

What should you do if you find yourself fencing against a beginner who continually beats your blade? One simple maneuver is to drop your blade to the seventh or eighth position, thereby making it difficult for your blade to be hit. A somewhat more difficult but perhaps more rewarding tactic would be to avoid the beat by dropping your point just under the beat, and making a disengage attack.

Remember, *fencing is a thinking person's game,* and merely waving your blade around as you hop in and out of distance takes no brains at all. Make plans, even if they are simple, and try to carry them out.

Before a practice bout I recommend that the beginning fencer consciously decide just what specific, learned attacks and parries to work on. Will it be simple attacks from perfect distance, or beat disengage attacks, for instance? Whatever you decide to do, work on it until you improve those particular actions. This type of practice is more challenging and, therefore, more fun than aimless slashing and bashing practice.

This is an exciting sport in which two people vie for position as they try to find weaknesses in each other's attack and defense. Enjoy the battle as you work to gain confidence and as your fencing improves.

Evaluation Question

What action do the fencers take after each of the following situations: the blade tip touches the opponent's chest; the tip touches the thigh and then the torso; the tip grazes the legal target?

Notes

1. *Fencing Rules,* 1991 ed. (Colorado Springs, CO: United States Fencing Association, Inc.) Article 31.

Techniques for the More Advanced Fencer

5

When you have acquired the ability to perform basic techniques well, you can progress to more advanced techniques that will provide greater variety for your game.

Advanced Footwork

Crossover Advance

This is a variation that covers a little more distance than the regular advance or retreat. The forward crossover is done by crossing the back foot forward, in front of the forward foot, so it is placed ahead of the leading foot with the heel directly in front of the leading toe, then quickly advancing the front foot so that your feet end in the proper guard position.

This may be used to gain distance toward a retreating fencer, or it may be followed by an advance-lunge attack against a retreating fencer. It is important that the body remain in an upright, balanced guard position during this maneuver. It must be done very quickly and smoothly (see fig. 5.1).

Crossover Retreat

This may be used for a quick retreat that also covers a little more distance than the standard retreat. The front foot crosses behind the rear foot and the front toe is placed directly behind the back heel; then the back foot quickly moves backward to the proper guard position. This action may be combined with retreats or may be followed by a flèche attack that is described later in this chapter. Body balance and control are essential during the crossover footwork in order to be constantly prepared to defend oneself or take advantage of an opportunity to attack (see fig. 5.2).

Jump Forward or Backward

The jump is yet another method of gaining or giving ground. To jump forward, the front foot should reach forward as the push for the jump is made from the back foot. Both feet should land at the same time in the normal guard position. This is faster than a regular advance and can be combined with other footwork.

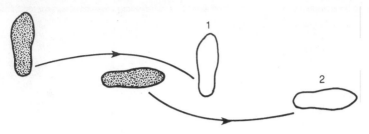

Figure 5.1
Forward crossover advance; the shaded footprints represent the starting position.

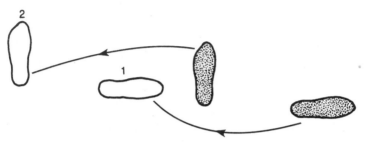

Figure 5.2
Crossover retreat; the shaded footprints represent the starting position.

To jump backward, reach backward with the rear foot while pushing back with the front foot. As with the forward jump, both feet should land at the same time and in the normal guard position. Body control must be maintained at all times.

It is important that the feet just skim the surface of the floor. It is a mistake to jump up more than absolutely necessary because the action will be slower, more obvious, and some point control will inevitably be lost.

The Ballestra

The ballestra is a jump-lunge. It is faster than an advance-lunge because there are two motions instead of the three required to advance, then lunge. It begins with the forward jump that is described above while extending the foil arm. The back foot should land about where the forward foot was before moving. This jump is followed by a lunge, using the front toes to add impetus to the lunge as they contact the floor after the jump. There should be little upward motion as you skim the surface of the strip.

The ballestra is most often used with a two-part attack, such as a beat-disengage, or a one-two. It is useful for a shorter fencer who must take an extra step to reach a taller fencer, or against a fencer who habitually retreats out of attacking distance. It will not catch a fencer who retreats several times unless preceded by several quick advances, in which case you can catch a quickly retreating fencer.

Figure 5.3
Flèche, or running attack. (Photo by Ric Thompson)

Common Errors

1. Jumping too high. Skim the floor.
2. Trying to jump too far, thereby slowing the attack. Jump as far as an advance would take you.
3. Failing to begin the attack with the jump. Extend your arm or beat as the jump begins.

The Flèche

The *flèche,* or running attack, is an advanced skill that can be effective if used sparingly. It is a swift attack that must be made very suddenly, with no telegraphing motion, so that it will surprise the opponent. It can be described as a do-or-die attack since it is an all-out attack in which the attacker runs past the other fencer in an attempt to score. To do this, extend your arm as you drive your body forward with the right toe, then lead forward with the left foot, which passes beyond the right foot to continue running past your opponent. The attacker must run past, never into, the other fencer, for this could be dangerous to both fencers and is clearly forbidden in the rules of fencing. The attacker must allow the sword arm to relax with the hit to lessen the danger of breaking the blade. If this attack fails, the attacker may not continue fencing because action must stop as soon as one fencer passes another, although the defender may make an immediate riposte as the attacker runs past.

The flèche should not be made from much more than fencing distance. As the body moves forward in a near horizontal plane, the hit should arrive before taking the second step. A longer running attack is easily defended against. This is not a substitute for the lunge as some lazy fencers tend to believe, but a separate tactic that should be saved for special moments.

The flèche should never be made against an opponent who is inclined to attack or advance into an attack. It is best made against an opponent who likes to retreat. It should not be used often since its main advantage lies in surprise, and the attacker is unable to stop or change direction once the attack has begun.

Attacks to the Blade

Any action that deflects the opponent's blade from the target, thereby clearing the way for an attack, is an attack to the blade. The beat and press were discussed in chapter 2, but there are two additional attacks to the blade that should be mentioned. The *bind* and the *croise* are very useful actions that remove a menacing point and, if properly done, continue to score.

The Bind

The bind is made only against an extended arm with a menacing point. The opponent's extended arm should be fairly rigid so the entire arm and sword act as a lever. This action carries the opponent's blade from high line to low line, where the attacker attempts to score with a touch made in opposition to the blade, thereby assuring the attacker protection during this action. To make a bind, meet the feeble of the other blade with the forte of your own blade in four or six. If it is taken in four, your point is guided over the other blade and downward to score in the line of eight. From an engagement of six, the blade would pass over and downward to the position of seven. Your arm should extend as your point crosses the other blade. The action must be quickly done in one strong motion so that the other person's foil will be controlled throughout the attack.

If very powerfully done, this action can be used successfully to disarm an opponent, but there is no advantage in doing so because action stops when a foil is dropped.

Evaluation Question

It is advantageous in dueling to disarm the opponent. Is this also true in fencing? Why or why not?

Defense Against the Bind

Because the bind can only be made against a straight arm, defense against the bind consists of bending the foil arm to parry in seven or eight, depending on which side the attack is arriving. If the attacker is not quick enough or telegraphs the intent to bind, it is not difficult to evade the attempt to bind by passing the point underneath the attacker's blade, arm still extended and point in line. If the attacker does not meet the other blade, he or she does not gain right-of-way, which remains with the extended arm.

Common Errors

1. Failure to engage the blade in four or six before trying to bind. If you try to take the blade while going over it, you have already advertised the fact that you are making the bind. This attack requires a subtle approach so that you almost caress the other blade; then take control with the bind before the other fencer knows what is happening.
2. Beating the blade as you try to engage it. Sneak up on it.
3. Turning your hand into pronation during the attack. As the sword hand turns palm down, your blade will change position so that you lose the necessary opposition to the other blade.

The Croise

The croise is made in much the same way as the bind, but it is made against a straight-arm attack that brings the other blade so close to your target that a complete bind is dangerous in that it brings the other blade across your body. If the opponent is close, the croise is better to use than the bind because it moves from the engagement of four to seven, or from six to eight. This is like a half-bind, still made with opposition and control of the other blade.

Tactical Variations of the Offense

Change of Tempo

The list of attacks discussed in chapter 3 need not be expanded, but these attacks may be varied effectively by changing the timing used in their execution. In the one-two or double, for instance, you can make a definite, but slightly slower, longer feint than usual followed by a sudden burst of speed as you make the final disengage, thereby upsetting the timing of the defense. This principle can be effectively applied to any attack. The feint may be explosively fast or a very subtle, sliding action that is deceptively slow.

Counter Attacks

Counter attacks are offensive actions made into attacks.

The *stop thrust* is a straight thrust, with or without a lunge, depending on the distance the thrust must travel to hit, into the opponent's attack or advance. It should be made only when the adversary withdraws the sword arm so that the stop arrives before the final action of the attack begins. If properly made, the stop will usually prevent the attack from hitting.

The stop is never a defense against a well-executed attack, but it takes right-of-way from an imperfect attack in certain instances. As long as an attack, even an imperfect one, continues in a forward direction, it must be considered right unless there is a definite withdrawal or hesitation of the sword arm between actions of a composed attack. It should be used sparingly since the attack almost always has

Figure 5.4
A stop thrust with oppostiton. The attacker's blade is deflected as the stop is made. (Photo by David Cary)

right-of-way over a stop thrust. In the case of a double hit the decision as to who is right rests with the director, who may understandably have difficulty in accurately analyzing confusing actions.

The *stop with opposition* is similar to the stop thrust but is safer because the thrust is made with opposition that closes the line of attack. The stop with opposition is usually made against a compound attack. It should be timed so that the stop is made during the final thrust of a one-two or a double. If the thrust is to the sixth line, a simple extension with opposition should be made to the opponent's right shoulder. If the thrust is to the fourth line, the extension should be made with opposition in four.

False Attack

The false attack is similar to a feint and is used for the same reasons, but it is made with a partial or full lunge. It must look like an attack, but it is intended to fall just short. It is done to provoke a response from the opponent that will, in turn, lead to the conclusion of the attack with a parry riposte.

Counter-Time Attack

This is often referred to as a "second intent" attack. In the case described above, the conclusion of the attack that follows the initial false attack is a counter-time attack. Any preparatory action, such as a feint or beat, that draws a parry-riposte or stop thrust, may be followed by an immediate parry and counter riposte. The beauty of starting a counter-time attack with a false attack is that the attacker's point is very close to the intended target because the attacker has lunged.

This attack may be made either offensively or defensively and is particularly effective. Timing must be precise, and to do this action effectively takes a great deal of practice, but the results are worth it.

When you fence against a person who makes counter-time attacks, a good defense is to retreat and make a decisive, blocking parry. If, however, you suspect such an attack, you may refuse to react to the preliminary feint and wait for the final action before parrying.

Evaluation Question

If your opponent is known to make counter-time attacks, what defensive moves would be good to try in response?

Parry Two (Second)

Some fencers prefer the parry of two over parry eight. This parry also protects the low-outside line, but it is a pronation parry. That is, the parry is made with the palm of the foil hand down instead of up, as it would be when parrying eight.

To make this parry, rotate the wrist down so that the foil is in the same position as it would be with the parry of eight. You must be careful to do this without lifting the elbow which is a common fault that exposes the right flank to your opponent.

I prefer the parry of eight in most cases because it is a smaller motion and leaves your hand in a better position for most ripostes. The second parry does lend itself to a riposte to another right-handed fencer's right flank, with the hand still in pronation. This parry may also be useful when a right-handed fencer goes against a left-handed one because a riposte to the front, or outside lines, of the left-handed fencer may be effectively made with a pronated hand. In both of these cases, the parry is made with the palm down and in position for the riposte.

The Riposte

The **riposte** is an offensive action made by a fencer who has parried an attack. The riposte may be simple or compound and may be made to any line. It may be made with a lunge if the opponent recovers to his guard position quickly, or it may be made by thrusting without a lunge if it is made quickly enough to arrive before the opponent has had time to recover to the guard position.

An *immediate riposte* rebounds from the parry to score with a very fast direct thrust.

A *delayed riposte* is made after momentarily holding the parry, usually to riposte with a disengage or cutover that is made as the opponent's arm returns to the defensive guard position. The delayed riposte may be made with compound attacks, but often these are very time consuming so that, except to surprise the opponent by changing tactics, the simple ripostes tend to be more successful.

A *counter riposte* may be made in just the same way by the fencer who has successfully parried a riposte.

Ripostes may either be made with or without opposition. In a simple opposition riposte you would riposte with your hand in the same line as the parry. For

Figure 5.5
A riposte without opposition.

instance, as you parry in four your hand moves to the left of your target. To riposte with opposition your hand should remain in four as you extend your arm to riposte so that your opponent's blade will be kept outside of your target. This type of parry is valuable against a fencer who continues an attack after it has been parried.

To riposte without opposition from, for instance, a crisp parry of four, you would move your hand across your body to riposte in six with your hand reaching in front of your right shoulder. This is apt to be a little slower because your hand moves farther as it crosses your body to score, but it is a good tactic against a fencer who can be relied upon to go on the defensive as soon as an attack is parried. By changing to a different line you force your opponent to make a wide parry.

Common Errors

1. Moving too close to the attacker, making it difficult to aim for a riposte.
2. Hesitating momentarily when making a direct riposte. A direct riposte should rebound from the parry to the target.
3. Extending the arm before aiming. Aim, extend, and then touch.

The Remise

The remise is an offensive action made by the attacker who has failed to hit on the first attempt. It is a second action that places the point on the target without

Figure 5.6
A riposte made with opposition in four to close the line on the side threatened by the attacker.
(Photo by David Cary)

changing line and without withdrawing the arm. The remise may be made when the opponent parries but does not riposte, or when the riposte is delayed or composed. In order to take right-of-way, it must score before the final action of the riposte, if any, begins.

When one fences a person who effectively uses the remise, immediate simple ripostes are best because such ripostes have the legal right-of-way over a remise, whereas a delayed or compound riposte does not. On the other hand, when an opponent usually returns to the guard position after his attack has been parried, the delayed or compound riposte may be more effective.

Fencing with the Electric Foil

Since fencing is a combat sport, it is natural that participants should seek competition with others once they have learned to use the basic skills effectively. Because most competitive fencing has been electrically scored since the 1955 World Championships, a word should be said about fencing with the electrical foil.

The electric scoring apparatus is designed to determine hits made on a fencer more accurately than the average judge can. The fencer's personal equipment consists of an electric foil, a body cord, a jacket, an underarm protector, and a lamé vest that exactly covers the valid target and is worn over the regular fencing jacket.

Figure 5.7
Electric scoring machine and reels. Reel (A); scoring machine (B); body cord attachment (C).
(Photo by David Cary)

The electric foil has a special point mounted on the end of the blade. The point is separated from its base by a spring that is depressed when a direct hit is made, causing the scoring apparatus to register a hit, valid or invalid. A thin wire is connected to the point and runs down a groove along the length of the blade to a plug on the inside of the guard. One end of the body cord plugs into the weapon, and the other connects with the signaling apparatus.

The signaling apparatus includes two reels and a scoring machine. A fencer plugs the body cord into the reel cord, one behind each end of the strip. The reel in turn attaches to the scoring machine by means of an electrical cord. Each fencer is able to advance or retreat for the length of the strip as the reel cord unwinds and winds again with little resistance, by means of a spring that is in each reel.

The signaling machine is equipped with a buzzer, which gives an auditory signal for a hit and two lights for each fencer. Whenever the lamé vest is hit, either a red or green light flashes, depending on which fencer has scored. If a hit arrives off target, it is indicated by a white light.

Anyone who intends to fence competitively should practice with an electric foil or with a dummy electric blade, which feels like an electric weapon but is less expensive for everyday use.

The first electric weapons were much heavier than the standard or nonelectric foil. Consequently, point control was seriously affected, and for awhile it seemed that the methods of attack and defense would have to be modified. Weapons have been improved, however, so that, while there is still a difference in weight, the standard techniques are nonetheless possible. The difference is in the feel of the blade, which tends to be a little point-heavy. The point tends to whip more, which means that control is even more important than with the standard foil. A wide parry with the electric foil will travel farther and take longer to correct than when executed with a standard foil, so more precision is required. When using à standard foil, it is best to parry with the forte, or stronger part of the blade. An electric blade has more weight ncar the point than a standard one, and parries may be made nearer the center of the blade. This is advantageous because there will be less lateral whipping of the point when impact against the other blade occurs somewhat nearer the tip; therefore, controlling the point will be a little easier.

Fencers used to keep their points at eye level to provide a strong defense, but with the heavier point, the chin-high guard previously described is preferred by most people, for it makes for greater accuracy and speed in the attack or riposte.

The electric foil has made touches to the eighth (low-outside) line very effective, for some fencers have difficulty in defending this line. If a defender lifts the elbow to parry in eight, a common fault, that line is further opened, and chances of deceiving that parry are also increased. Low line attacks are often frustrating in standard foil when judges call the touches because touches to the back are often obscured from their line of vision and go unnoticed.

To register a touch, the electric foil must arrive so that more than 500 grams of pressure are exerted on the tip. Before every competition and sometimes every bout, the foil should be tested by placing a 500-gram test weight, designed for this purpose, on the tip of the vertical foil. The tip should not be depressed until a light tap activates the circuit, after which the spring inside it should return the tip to its extended position. Fencers need not hit hard enough to bend the blade very much, and the hit need not remain on the target for the benefit of judges, so the attacker can, and should, be prepared to quickly go to the defense if necessary after touching, or to hit again immediately if there is no immediate riposte. Some fencers have a tendency to stop and look at the scoring machine when a point should have landed, but unless the point lands squarely (a point might land slightly sideways, or the fencers may be too close and bend the blade too much so that the pressure is on the edge of the tip), the machine will not register a touch, and the fencer who stops to look at the machine may be scored against easily if the previous touch did not activate it. For this reason, a fencer should keep fencing until the director halts the bout, so a quick remise is preferable to stopping to wait for a halt. Obviously, the proper distance is very important.

Evaluation Question

Why is it especially important when fencing with an electric foil to maintain proper distance from the opponent?

Infighting

Infighting occurs when two fencers are closer than fencing distance to each other. It is important to practice infighting techniques so you will not be at a loss when you need this skill. While it is desirable to maintain proper fencing distance, there are inevitably times when fencers must continue actions at close quarters. The need for infighting may occur accidentally when both fencers advance or attack at the same time, but, unfortunately, some fencers favor infighting and systematically close their distance in order to gain the advantage of using a style they prefer against a more conventional fencer who may not be as effective in such close quarters.

It is fairly easy to defend oneself at close quarters because your opponent's actions must be large. If you do not panic you will find it is not difficult to parry until the director calls "halt." When you see a clear shot, take it, but remember you will be vulnerable, so make a fast jab to score. The back is a favorable target for infighters and is difficult to defend although a high parry can be effective.

The thing you should not do is retreat when an opponent closes distance because then you will retreat into the opponent's range where you can easily be touched. It is better to keep a firm stance or run past the infighter, at which time fencing must stop because you are not allowed to fence in reversed positions. There is no penalty for passing the other fencer as long as you remain on the strip.

Foil fencing has suffered from the overuse of infighting, so that action is often very confusing and bouts have often turned into mere jabbing contests. As a result members of the international rules committee have turned their attention to remedying this problem. Officials have been instructed to be much more strict in enforcing the rules regarding right-of-way as well as general conduct of the bout.

The results are beginning to be rewarding on the international level. Officials are insisting that the sword arm be extended at the start of an attack, whereas for several years almost any attack, no matter how poorly executed, had right-of-way. Foil fencing is again becoming cleaner, with clear actions that can be more easily analyzed than during the years of messy fencing.

Infighting is seen less often as a result of the application of the rules that have been on the books but loosely interpreted.

Suggested Readings

Alaux, Michel. *Modern Fencing*. New York: Charles Scribner's Sons, 1975.
Campos, Jules. *The Art of Fencing*. New York: Vantage Press, 1989.
Lukovich, Istvan. *Fencing*. Hungary: Alföldi Printing House, Debrecen, 1986. Rev. by John Harvie, Newbury Books, 1986.
Pitman, Brian. *Fencing Techniques of Foil, Epee and Sabre*. U.K.: Crowood, 1989.
Shaff, Jo. *Fencing*. New York: Atheneum, 1982.
Simmonds, A. T., and Morton, E. D. *Start Fencing*. U.K.: Sportsmans Press, 1990.

Psychological and Physical Conditioning for Fencing

6

Psychological Preparation for Competition

Much attention is now being given to the mental and psychological aspects of training as well as to the physical and technical preparation necessary for optimum results in all sports, including fencing. For many years the Eastern European countries have spent much time and money in researching this area of competitive preparation. The United States began serious, organized research in this field in the late 1960s and early 1970s.

Setting Goals

The first thing for serious students of fencing to do is to set realistic short-term goals that are appropriate for them in terms of their attained level of skill and physical condition. Then fencers must conscientiously train to achieve specific technical and physical levels that will lead to optimum performances.

Once short-term goals are reached, new, higher goals must be set so that there is always something to work toward. It is not realistic for a beginning fencer to plan to make an Olympic team as a first goal, because that is so far in the future that there is nothing immediate or tangible to work toward and very little by which to gauge progress. One needs short-term goals along the way so that hard work will lead to definite, observable successes as improvement occurs. An Olympic goal may serve as a long-range dream that can provide necessary motivation while working toward short-term goals.

Concentration and Focus

During practice training sessions it is important to have a clear and precise plan for what is to be achieved. If certain attacks are to be perfected, then a fencer must focus on using those specific actions. Concentration is necessary to ensure the moves will be made from the correct distance, at the correct time, and in the correct manner. The desired action must be done again and again in both a structured and nonstructured way. In a training session with the instructor the action will be done repetitively in a structured way until it is performed well. While practicing in a bouting situation the same actions are done in a nonstructured way because the fencing partner, or opponent, will make attacks and parries that are not predictable in terms of actions, timing, and distance. It takes great concentration and self-discipline to keep to the desired actions in order to work specifically on the task of the moment. In such practice, winning the bout is not as important as gaining the goal of making this attack or defense really work for you.

During competitive fencing the habits of concentration that are developed during practice are really put to the test. It is important to have a game plan and to concentrate on your plan throughout the bout. If external irritations or distractions occur, they must be put aside and concentration and focus regained in order to perform to the best of one's ability. All a person can really expect is to do one's best at any given time. For instance, if a person feels a referee made a bad decision that cost an important score, it is too easy to waste valuable time during a bout feeling resentful or angry about an unfavorable call. While focusing on emotional reactions to such a situation, attention is diverted from the real issue at hand. The call went the wrong way so what can you do to see that the mistake is not repeated? Free your mind from outside pressures and focus on your performance, not on the outcome of a bout. Make clearer actions, or change tactics. Learn what kinds of actions a particular official rewards and use them.

Worry raises the anxiety level, saps energy, and generally hinders performance and focus on the job to be done. While thinking about strategy and tactics it is important to ask yourself *how* you will score a point or successfully defend against an attack, rather than wondering *if* you will be able to do it. Posing the *if* question to yourself sets up a negative concept that admits the possibility of failure and introduces a degree of tension and doubt that will certainly affect performance. Keep to positive self-suggestions that will reinforce your game plan.

Mental Warm-Up

Mental warm-up can be as important as a physical warm-up. It is important to feel positive about the event confronting you. You should imagine yourself moving as you have been taught to move. Imagine your perfect attack scoring and your precise parry ripostes finding your opponent's target. This sort of mental preparation should get the adrenalin moving and get you a little bit excited about the task to be done.

According to Cratty, "The more a task requires "pure" skill, in contrast to elements of power, endurance, and the like, the more likely it will be that mental practice will be useful."[1] As you mentally go through steps of skilled movement you should see yourself performing *specific* actions. In using mental imagery to practice against a *specific* opponent, try to see yourself reacting to *specific* actions you expect the other person to make. Better yet, you may see yourself setting up that fencer to react as you wish.

Physical Excitement

Your body responds to anticipated stress with excitement. Cox refers to this excitement as "arousal."[2] Adrenalin flows, the pulse quickens, and breathing accelerates as you prepare to compete.

How much arousal is beneficial to a competitor and at what point does such arousal become detrimental? Under competitive situations we know that too low a level of emotional excitement leads to a "flat" performance. On the other hand, too high a level of excitement disrupts concentration and can also lead to fatigue due to greater energy consumption.[3]

If you are overly excited with dozens of "butterflies" in your stomach, you will need to calm yourself to an appropriate level of arousal. This can be done by controlled slow and deep breathing and by practicing relaxation techniques. Relaxation is a learned skill just as any other skill that is acquired by practice as you develop an awareness of your body. One common technique is to tense your muscles and hold this tension for several seconds. Then consciously relax your body, segment by segment. Starting with the top of the head, progress to relaxing facial muscles and progress to the neck, right arm and fingers, left arm and fingers, torso, right leg, and left leg. It is important to recognize the difference between tension and relaxation in order to be able to go from one state to the other at will.

It is also possible to reduce a measure of arousal by reinforcing yourself with positive cues. "I will do my best." "I have trained well." "I will follow my game plan." These are examples of ways to bolster the self-confidence necessary to lessen the fear element. A degree of fear and anxiety can be useful in bouts of short duration, less so in contests of prolonged duration.

It has been found that highly skilled athletes need more arousal for simple tasks than less skilled athletes do in performing a complex task.

Evaluation Question

Why do you suppose that highly skilled athletes need more arousal for simple tasks than less skilled athletes do for complex tasks?

Self-Assessment

A review of what you have learned from a practice session can be very valuable. Could you have been faster or more precise? What did you learn and what must you do about that knowledge? What aspects of the practice session were you particularly pleased with? What felt good and why? Such mental sessions help to reinforce the good and identify that which is less than wonderful for further work.

After a competition you must ask the same questions. How was my performance, how can I improve, and what did I learn?

Physical Preparation for Fencing

Today's mobile game of fencing imposes varying demands on the fencer, depending on whether one is a beginning fencer or a high-level competitor. Fencing is a vigorous activity that requires cardiorespiratory efficiency, strength, flexibility, and speed. "Cardiorespiratory endurance is defined as the ability to perform large-muscle, dynamic, moderate-to-high intensity exercise for prolonged periods."[4]

Figure 6.1
Leg and torso stretch, reaching right, then left.

Figure 6.2
Leg and torso stretch. (Photo by David Cary)

Increasing Leg Strength

Fencers need to work to develop the ability to make explosive action with their legs. Quickness and strength are the goals here. Running up stairs, preferably two at a time, is one excellent exercise to increase leg strength and endurance. One of the best ways to achieve these goals is to practice fencing footwork. Advance, retreat, and lunge for extended periods of time.

Interval training is valuable in this kind of exercise. This means that you should drill vigorously for a relatively short period of time, paying strict attention to proper form of the actions practiced. After a short rest, repeat the exercise period, rest, exercise, and so on. The advantage of this type of training is that by stopping before your form begins to get sloppy, you will not be reinforcing improper actions.

Inevitably as you tire, you use your muscles in a slightly different way, and this is when you begin to practice and reinforce incorrect movement patterns. To increase strength and endurance through interval training, you will need to drill for more work intervals. As you improve, you will be able to work for slightly longer intervals as endurance and strength increase.

Increasing Flexibility

Good flexibility is needed to enable you to move as necessary in any given situation without putting undue strain on ligaments or muscles and tendons. You want to avoid putting stress on joints as they reach their maximum range of motion. Therefore, you should exercise to increase your range of motion. The stretching exercises in figures 6.1–6.8 will effectively increase the mobility of joints using ten repetitions of each exercise, holding each stretch three to five seconds.

In figures 6.1–6.8 you will see the fencer first stretching in a position where it is possible to isolate specific body parts. This is more easily attainable in the sitting position. In this position the influence of gravity will not affect balance,

Figure 6.3
Leg and torso stretch, reaching right, then left.

Figure 6.4
Pretzel, stretching torso and hip areas.
(Photo by David Cary)

Figure 6.5
Groin stretch. Elbows push down on knees.
(Photo by David Cary)

Figure 6.6
Back and shoulder stretch. The head must be held up in order to do this correctly.
(Photo by David Cary)

and therefore the fencer can concentrate on the stretch. Standing positions elicit certain reflexes that tend to hinder rather than facilitate the development of increased range of motion.

Once an adequate amount of flexibility is developed, the fencer must leave the sitting position and get into a position that more closely resembles the movements to be used while fencing. Sport participants need to progress in their development of flexibility in positions that specifically match the movement demands put on them during performance. This is consistent with the principle that the body specifically adapts to the demands that are imposed on it. This is known as the SAID PRINCIPLE ("specific adaptation to imposed demands," first so stated by Logan and McKinney). It has been shown that when flexibility is needed in certain positions, it is best to train for flexibility in these specific positions.[5]

An important aspect of stretching is that all such exercises must be done slowly and evenly. Avoid brisk, bobbing motions that tend to tighten the muscle rather than relax it because of the stretch reflex in the muscle being stretched.

Figure 6.7
Standing hamstring and torso stretch, to left center, and right, contracting abdominal muscles. (Photo by David Cary)

Figure 6.8
Hamstring stretch. (Photo by David Cary)

Another key principle in stretching is to always contract the muscle opposite to the one being stretched. For example, in figure 6.1, the fencer is stretching his lower trunk and hamstring muscles while he is also actively contracting his abdominals and anterior hip muscles as he flexes his toes upward. This enhances relaxation of the posterior hip trunk and leg muscles being stretched.

Always work to go a little bit farther than you did last time if you wish to increase flexibility. However, if you are sore the following day your body is telling you that you stretched too far or too much. Stretching should be done daily. To maintain what flexibility you have, just stretch to your attained limit without increasing the range of motion you have achieved. It is important that you exercise regularly to maintain what you have gradually achieved or you will have to start all over again.

You will find that through fencing you can achieve a high level of physical conditioning that can help you in other endeavors.

Improving Speed and Accuracy

To improve speed and accuracy of movement so that instantaneous responses to sudden actions will be well executed, rather than large and uncontrolled, the fencer must concentrate on perfecting actions, and must repeat them again and again until perfect motions are automatic. Although you often will react to a sudden threat on a subcortical level, you will just as often choose your actions, and you should have to decide only which movement to make, not how to execute it. The "how" must be made automatic through repetition.

To gain maximum improvement, the fencer should practice speed and accuracy of a skill simultaneously. In order to establish exactly how a move should be made, an action may be practiced in slow motion, but once an action is understood, it should be practiced at full but controlled speed. This will develop speed along with accuracy.

The lunge, for instance, must be performed powerfully if a fencer is practicing to attack more effectively. Once you have lunged at full speed, stay in the lunge position long enough to make sure that all parts of your body are correctly aligned. If they are not, correct your position and repeat the lunge again and again until you are satisfied that it is well executed. When you reach this point, practice an immediate recovery from the full lunge to the guard position. You may then progress to the advance-lunge, recover, retreat, and so forth, all of which can be practiced in the same manner.

Notes

1. Cratty, Bryant, *Psychological Preparation and Athletic Excellence* (New York: Movement Publications Inc., 1984), 25.
2. Cox, Richard H., *Sport Psychology,* 2d ed. (Dubuque, IA: Wm. C. Brown Publishers, 1990), 99.
3. Cox, Richard H., *Sport Psychology,* 2d ed., (Dubuque, IA: Wm. C. Brown Publishers), 99.
4. Breit, Nicholas, Professor of Kinesiology and Physical Education, California State University, Northridge, from a 1989 interview.
5. Breit, Nicholas, "The Effects of Body Position and Stretching Technique on the Development of Hip and Back Flexibility." (Ph.D diss., Springfield College, Springfield, MA, 1977)

Bouting for the More Advanced Fencer

7

There is much more to skillful bouting than good, basic technique. There is not so much more to know, but to use these techniques forcefully, confidently, and wisely is an important difference between skilled and mediocre performances.

When your technical skill has progressed sufficiently, you will want to test your ability against another fencer of equal or superior ability in bouting and competitive situations. Bouting is a true test of your speed, power, timing, and the ability to control your emotions and body; of your ability to analyze another fencer; and of your ingenuity. You are completely on your own, and you will win or lose depending on how well you apply your knowledge. You often will need to make split-second decisions and decisively carry them out.

Whether you are engaged in informal bouting practice or in a tournament, you must try to score with the same determination, or you will do a disservice to yourself and to your opponent. Neither of you will benefit from a half-hearted attempt to attack or defend. In informal bouting, however, you are more free to experiment and to use attacks and defenses that you have been practicing. In competitive fencing you must use actions in which you have gained confidence during practice sessions. The harder you have worked, and the more you have experimented in practice bouting, the more choice of action you will have to select from in a tournament situation.

The main problem in bouting with another person is deciding what to do and when to do it. This chapter attempts to answer these questions. In a contest between two otherwise evenly matched fencers, the bout will go to the one who more effectively outthinks the other. You must always be aware of your own responses to probing actions made by your opponent. You should try not to respond to feints unless you choose to invite an attack in order to set up an action for yourself, and you must avoid any repetitious actions such as a continual change of engagement in advance or patterns of beating without a definite plan in mind. Be aware of every move you make, know why you make it, and watch your opponent's reaction to what is learned about you.

Laying Your Strategy

The first thing you will probably do when you face another fencer is to test for responses. You must find out how fast one moves, how large or small one's actions are, how one tends to react, what kinds of traps will work, and what kinds will be laid for you. If you fence against a person you know very well, you must still learn how that person feels today.

There are a number of ways to discover what you want to know so that you can plan your tactic according to what the other person is likely to do. This preliminary testing must be sudden and convincing in order to draw a true response from your opponent, who is probably trying to find out the same things about you.

Probable Responses to a Feint or False Attack

There are several responses you can draw from a feint or false attack:

1. A parry response, with or without a riposte, means that a one-two or double, depending on whether a direct or counter parry was used, will be a logical choice of attacks.
2. If a strong feint brings no response at all, your opponent is probably well controlled and will not parry until certain that you intend to hit with a direct attack. In this instance, try an explosive direct attack to score. If it succeeds, try the same thing again until it fails. If it is parried, how did your opponent parry it? You are again ready for a one-two or double, but it will be more difficult to time against a delayed parry. You will need a deep feint with a last-minute evasion of the parry.
3. A retreat with or without a parry may indicate that an advance attack will be necessary for your proposed attack to reach. Plan an advance attack that will deceive any defensive attempts.
4. An extension into your feint tells you that you can expect your opponent to make stop thrusts. You can precede a straight thrust or disengage with a beat to either side of the blade to gain clear right-of-way. You can also effectively make a second-intent attack in which you make a false attack, parry the stop, and continue to hit.

Responses to a Beat or Press

You can beat lightly on either side of the blade or press in the line of engagement to discover how your opponent reacts. He or she may

1. Make an answering beat or press, in which case you may beat or press and make a disengage or a one-two, timing the feint, or disengage so that the answering beat or press will not find your blade and the opponent will be forced to go for a parry. If you are faster than the other fencer, a disengage may work, but if your opponent parries well, a one-two will be better. You have set up a lateral movement with your preliminary action.
2. Make no response, which means that a strong beat-straight thrust may score. After being hit in this manner, the opponent will parry a strong feint of a straight thrust so that you can set up your deceptive attacks.
3. Attack as you beat or press. You can then "invite" a fencer to attack by making a beat or press and then, since you are expecting the attack and will be ready, parry and riposte.

Evaluation Question

Discuss with a less experienced fencer the importance of "thinking ahead."

Responses to a Change of Engagement

With or without an advance, a change of engagement may reveal something about your opponent, who may

1. Change the hand position to protect the line that you have changed. You may change engagement and then make a disengage or one-two as your opponent's hand moves to protect the line to which you have moved; again, this will set up a lateral response on the part of the other fencer. You can vary this action by making the attack to the low line.
2. Change engagement to the original line. You may change, then make a derobement, which is a counter disengage that avoids an opponent's change. If the opponent parries this, avoid by disengaging again to the high or low line.
3. Make a disengage attack. Any time you change, you must be ready to parry a possible derobement against you and then riposte. The fact that you are prepared for this possible attack gives you an advantage. A counter parry may be more effective than a direct parry because your opponent is more likely to try a one-two than a double in the event of a parry.
4. Not respond at all, in which case you may change, feint a glide to force a response, and deceive the parry. Caution is always necessary against someone who does not react to tentative maneuvers. Your opponent is probably planning to use such preliminary motions against you in the near future, so use variety and never set up a pattern of changing or beating unless you intend to invite an attack.

Responses to Simple Attacks or Beat Attacks

Often a sudden, explosive, unexpected attack can be enough of a surprise to be successful. If this works, try it again until it fails; then you will be ready for a composed attack to avoid whatever parry has been used to block the attack.

Varying Your Distance

It is best to move about on the strip, although it is not a bad idea to stop from time to time. However, if you stand for too long in one place you allow two things to happen: first, your opponent will have too much time to get set for an attack; second, a static position will tend to lessen your ability to move quickly and powerfully. By retreating or advancing before an attack your leg muscles will be better prepared to work for you so you will be ready to attack at all times. Any time you advance to within fencing distance, the opponent may attack and catch you slightly off balance and moving into the attack. To avoid this, extend your arm, beat-extend, or otherwise control the opponent's blade while advancing. However, change what you do during an advance to lessen the likelihood of having your actions anticipated. Never simply advance into a hit.

Figure 7.1
An all-out attack is parried by a retreating defender. (Photo by David Cary)

On the other hand, while advancing and retreating to varying distances, try to draw your opponent a little too close. Be completely alert in order to attack at the exact instant you see your opponent's toes rise to make an advance, allowing you to make an attack that you feel sure will land.

As a rule, you should retreat with a parry to add an extra margin of safety and to allow more time for defense. If you retreat too far though, it is difficult to reach with a riposte because of the extra distance between fencers. Through experience try to learn to retreat far enough so that your opponent's attack lands just short; then a half or full lunge with your riposte will be sufficient to reach.

Evaluation Question

Fencers are advised to move about on the strip. What are the dangers of standing too long in one place?

Attacks on Preparation

A good time to attack is while your opponent is preparing to attack, but before his or her attack actually begins. For instance, if you learn by observation that your opponent likes to make a beat or change engagement while advancing, you may make a disengage or a one-two that avoids an attempt to meet your blade as a fencer steps in. By making a bind you may take the initiative from a feint. Absolute concentration and alertness are necessary if you are to time an attack on preparation successfully. This is fun to do and a very exciting way to fence because the split-second timing required tends to keep you on your toes in order to detect any movement of which you can take advantage.

Figure 7.2
An attack-on-preparation. The fencer on the left is attacking into a careless advance.

Building Attack Sequences

Although it has been mentioned briefly, the possibility of progressing from simple to complex actions deserves special emphasis. To the degree that your opponent allows, you can lead him or her through a number of attacks and continue to build on defensive responses to previous attacks.

For instance, make a straight thrust, beat-straight thrust, disengage, or beat-disengage attack. Try to score; if you do, continue this attack until, in essence, you teach your opponent to parry it. You may advance, retreat, feint, or change engagement between attacks to divert your opponent's attention from your strategy. If you desire a direct parry to your direct attack, you are more likely to get it by attacking away from the other blade rather than with opposition because a counter parry is more difficult when it must be moderately wide. If your attack fails because your opponent, now convinced that you will continue to make simple attacks, parries with a direct parry, you can follow this up with a one-two attack. The one-two may be used, interspersed with diverting byplay, until it is parried with a second parry; then you may make the one-two by making the last action to the low line.

If your opponent switches to counter parries, you may similarly progress to a double attack.

Another sequence of attacks may begin with a cutover from the line of four to an open line of six. If you are engaged in four, you can make a simple cutover or a press cutover that may open the sixth line further if your opponent responds to the press with answering pressure. If you begin in six, you may change engagement to four and make the cutover as your opponent starts to close the fourth line. This is an effective attack and may well land. When the cutover is parried by a direct parry of six, you may feint a cutover and avoid the sixth parry to disengage low to the eighth line on your next attack. When this attack is parried, you may progress to a feint of cutover to eighth and disengage to the line of six as your opponent anticipates your attack to the low line.

There will be other byplay between attacks—try to keep the offensive by controlling the blade or changing distance, or you may go to the defense yourself. The time you pick to attack is important. The distance must be right, and you must catch your opponent who relaxes a little or whose attention wanders momentarily. You must surprise your opponent.

You may devise progressions of your own in this manner. One effective variation of this concept is to make a simple attack, then a two-part attack that changes line, and finally return to the first simple action when your second action is parried. The defender will be expecting a second action and will react little, if at all, to your feint; when this happens, turn the feint into the attack. It has been said that if all of a fencer's feints looked like attacks and all attacks looked like feints, one could always be a winner!

Setting Up Another Fencer

One of the most important ploys for a fencer to develop is the ability to set up an unsuspecting fencer for an attack or for a specific counterattack. If you must work to set up an unsuspecting fencer, that makes the game more interesting!

How do you lay traps? Actually there are so many possible ways to achieve this they cannot all be listed, nor do I pretend to know all of the possible deceptive ways to fool an opponent. A few such ideas are outlined below, however, just to present possibilities. You can perhaps expand on the ideas with tactics of your own.

Try to get an opponent to attack to a particular line by casually, and seemingly negligently, opening that line, particularly the high-outside line of six. If, on the other hand, you overtly open the line your opponent is surely going to say, "I am expected to attack to that open line. I will pretend to, then avoid the obvious parry that is being prepared for me." Or, "There is no way that I will fall into that trap," in which case the bait will not be taken. The idea is to make your invitations subtle if they are to really fool a fencer.

On the other hand, a blatant opening of a line will either keep a wary opponent from attacking at all, or set up a one-two attack against you, allowing you to make two parries and a riposte. The idea is always to keep one step ahead of the other person.

When a fencer makes feints against you to learn what your reactions are liable to be, why not give false clues? Deliberately parry, perhaps with a direct parry of four or six. When the ensuing attack against you actually arrives, parry with a counter parry and riposte. It is important that you make your false clues look like genuine reflexive responses.

Repetitive actions, made at a moderate speed, can lull an opponent to a false sense of security. For instance, beat (not too hard) and feint to an open line gently enough so that your opponent does not react to such an obvious feint. Repeat this same action several times as you slowly advance. You may feint to the same or different lines, but do not let it seem threatening. When you sense that your opponent is relaxing just a little too much, repeat the action, beat and slowly feint, then make a swift lunge to complete the attack. The slow feint should be fairly deep so there is little distance to travel to score against your relaxed opponent.

Similarly, you may make slow, deep, one-two false attacks that do not alarm the other fencer. Again, when the time and distance are correct, double the speed of the second part of the attack to score.

When an opponent gets wise to you and either takes the initiative in attacking, or is prepared for your change of pace, you may act interested in scoring to a particular line, only to make a serious attack to an opposite area. This can be particularly effective if you make several strong, wide actions to the line of four, then change to a quick attack to eight.

Once you get the idea, your possibilities are numerous. The guiding principle is to *never let your opponent know the full extent of your real intentions.*

The Left-Handed Fencer

Those fencers who are left-handed may have a psychological advantage over some opponents, and they will have a technical advantage over those who are unfamiliar with left-handed fencers. Right-handed fencers should fence with left-handers often to familiarize themselves with the differences that exist between left- and right-handed fencing. It may also be noted that left-handed fencers need to gain experience against other left-handed fencers for the same reasons. Most of their opposition will be with right-handed persons, so a left-handed fencer can be a problem to another left-hander.

Left-handers must develop a strong defense in the outside lines because this will be their most vulnerable area. When fencing right-handers, they will be in six, often a weaker line, when the right-hander is in the stronger line of four, and vice versa. A strong parry of six, counter six, and eight is especially important for both left- and right-handed fencers when they work against one another.

Evaluation Question

Which are the most vulnerable lines for a left-handed fencer bouting with a right-handed opponent? Which parries, in particular, should be strengthened for defense in this situation?

Very few inside attacks will succeed in this situation, but a feint to the inside followed by a disengage or cutover to the outside high or low line is an effective attack for either fencer. Accuracy is important here because the outside lines are smaller than those on the inside; however, they are more accessible.

Attacks on preparation may be effective if either fencer insists on engaging in either six or four. The attacker may change to the nonfavored line and make a derobement as the other fencer changes back to a preferred line.

Left-handed fencers often are frustrated when their well-planned, well-executed attacks slide across their intended target instead of solidly landing. Assuming that the aim and distance have been good, the most common reason for missing in this way is due to hand position when hitting. When hitting a fencer who is "other handed" than yourself, that is, left against right hand, turn the sword hand so that the blade bends into the target instead of away from it. To land on the inside lines in this instance, the hand should be slightly pronated, with the thumb knuckle at nine o'-clock. Similarly, when attacking the outside lines, the hand should be supinated, with the thumb knuckle at two or three o'clock.

Evaluation Question

If your opponent is "other-handed," how should you adjust your sword hand to hit? Where should the knuckles point to land on an outside line?

Suggested Counters to Common Systems of Fencing

There are many possible ways of dealing with various strategies. The important thing is to recognize a style for what it is and plan to use this knowledge to your own advantage. The following represent possible means of solving some common styles you may encounter:

1. Against a fencer who makes many stop or counter thrusts, you may succeed with second-intent (counter-time) attacks.
2. Against an opponent who refuses to attack, but who has a deadly parry riposte, you also may be successful with a second-intent attack that will bring about the desired attack for your parry and counter riposte.
3. Against a fencer who is always out of reach, you may make a ballestra attack, redouble to pursue the opponent, or retreat yourself to attack into an advance into your distance.
4. Against a fencer who wants to control your blade and who makes many beat attacks, you may fence with absence of the blade. If you take a low line guard, the opponent will be frustrated when attempting to take your blade. If your blade is followed to a low line with a fairly large action, you may take the initiative with a derobement to the high line. You may pretend to give a fencer your blade and counter disengage, avoiding the move to find your blade.
5. Against a person who always makes an advance attack or ballestra, you may upset the distance by occasionally holding your ground rather than retreating. Since this moving attack is calculated to reach a retreating defender, by holding your ground your attacker will not have reached the final phase of the attack by the time the distance to your target is closed, and the point will probably miss because the fencer will not be ready for the final thrust in time. The riposte after your parry will not be difficult because you know what the distance will be and can thrust accordingly.

6. Against bent-arm simple attacks, a stop thrust with opposition is effective. Against a poor compound attack, a stop thrust made *before the final action begins* can take the right-of-way. It is always safest to prevent the other person from hitting you in order to make sure you leave no doubt in an official's mind as to who scored. The safest move is stop thrust, then parry.

Hints for the Defense

Control is the watchword for the defender. You should watch the center of the target. You should not try to watch the point as it moves, for it will move too wide and too fast for the eye to follow. Nor should you try to follow movement of the hand with your eyes. If you watch a central point on the target, you will be able to see everything that develops with your peripheral vision. You will see any shoulder movements that may telegraph an attack, you will see where the hand moves, and you will be able to see foot movements without having to follow all of these movements with your eyes.

Try to parry only the real attacks, not the feints. The ability to tell a feint from an attack is acquired through experience, but the beginner can refuse to parry until the lunge actually develops. By delaying the parry, you give your opponent fewer clues, and you make compound attacks difficult to time. Ideally, you should parry just before the point lands, which takes a good eye, control, precision in the parry, and much practice.

Be sure to use variety in your defense, particularly against an experienced fencer. Mix the use of four and six and of direct and counter parries to make it difficult for the attacker to plan beat and feint attacks. It is virtually impossible to be flexible enough to react with a different action the instant an attack is launched against you, but once you have reacted to a parry, ask yourself what parry it was, and then plan how you will react to the next attack. You can program yourself to react in a certain way: you may take a second direct parry, a counter on the third, and continue to vary responses.

Defense Against a Riposte

Once you have initiated an attack, try to follow it to a successful touch, but if you hear or feel the steel of your opponent's blade as it parries yours, you must immediately go to the defense. Since a parry involves only the sword arm and blade, it can be made even if you are in the act of lunging or in a full lunge and cannot immediately return to the guard position. It is a mistake to feel you cannot defend until your body is out of the way because the arm and sword can move instantly if the elbow is not locked. It is difficult to establish this reaction, but with much practice it can become an automatic action. Against a good fencer who may do something other than make a direct riposte, a safe defense is to quickly parry in four and six or four-six-four to find the blade wherever it is.

Competitive Fencing

Whether you compete in a classroom tournament, an intercollegiate meet, or an amateur fencing meet, your mental approach to competition must be basically the same. Concentrate on how you intend to score without being scored upon as you fence. Take each point as it develops and do not worry about the total bout. You must, of course, know the score at all times and plan tactics around this knowledge, but think about what you are doing, *and why,* as you actually fence. You must realistically evaluate your situation and decide what your best tactics will be. Take a "this is what I must do" approach to each bout and each point.

If you are to fence a champion who is much better than you, you will realize the possibility of being defeated, but once the command "fence" is given and action starts, there should be no such thought in your mind. Think instead of what you will do. Your attention must be on distance, timing, and opportunities. Always give each bout your best effort.

If you are to compete against a beginning fencer, try to win every point. It is a mistake to give a weaker opponent two or three touches because these touches may be critical when it comes to advancing to the next round, or deciding a team victory.

As you begin to fence never ask yourself if you will win or lose. You will already have established doubt in your mind if you do and that can result in a slight loss of authority in the way you fence. Either you, or others, may apply pressure on the basis that you *must win* a given bout for one reason or another. Such pressure often diverts attention from the bout itself as a fencer thinks, "I must win," rather than, "*How will I score?*"

Take points one at a time. How will you score the next time, rather than considering how many points remain, is an important mental set. A common tactical mistake made by fencers who are leading by a good margin, such as four to zero or four to one, is to change their game at this point. This may be done to make the bout more interesting, because it seems that after four hits the other fencer will surely not be so gullible again, or because the leading fencer just wishes to play around. In any case, I have often seen such fencers lose a sure bout in just this way. *If a game is working, keep it going as long as it succeeds.*

Above all remember that there is something to be learned from each bout you fence and always give it your best effort.

Evaluation Question

Make yourself a brief list of the performance guidelines you should try to follow as you bout competitively.

Rules of Fencing

8

Fencing rules are established by the Federation Internationale d'Escrime (F.I.E.), the governing body of international fencing. These current rules, translated from French into English, are published in America by the United States Fencing Association (USFA).

The governing body of fencing in America was called the Amateur Fencers League of America from its inception until 1981 when it was renamed the United States Fencing Association.

This chapter contains an overview of the rules of fencing, and by no means represents a complete set of rules. Anyone who does compete must join the U.S. Fencing Association, must obtain an official rules manual, and become familiar with the rules. Information regarding joining the U.S. Fencing Association may be obtained from the USFA headquarters in Colorado Springs at the address listed on the last page of this chapter.

Field of Play

The foil strip (piste), may be of any nonslippery surface. All major electric tournaments should be fenced on a conductive, metallic surface. The strip is from 1.5 to 2 meters (5 ft. to 6 ft. 7 in.) wide and 14 meters (46 ft.) long. Seven lines should be drawn across the width of the strip: one center line; two on-guard lines—drawn 2 meters (6 ft. 7 in.) from each side of the center line; two end lines at the rear limit of the strip; and two warning lines marked 2 meters (6 ft. 7 in.) in from the end lines (see fig. 8.1).

Clothing

Fencers are responsible for their own safety. International rules require an all-white or solid pastel-colored uniform that provides maximum safety without sacrificing freedom of movement. However, in the United States, fencers may wear decorated uniforms at local, divisional, and sectional competitions. In addition, fencers at national events must have their last name in blue capital letters on the thigh of the non-weapon side, or on the back. The letters may not be taller than 10 cm (4").

The jacket must overlap the trousers at the waist by at least four inches when in the guard position. Fencers must wear an underarm protector in addition to the padded jacket, and women, are required to wear rigid breast protectors.

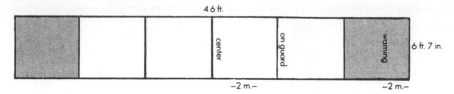

Figure 8.1
The foil strip (piste).

Men and women are required to wear trousers that fasten below the knee, which means that they may be the regulation knickers or ankle-length. White stockings are required when wearing knickers so that no bare skin is exposed on the legs. Fencers may be allowed to wear colored stockings in school meets to show their school colors.

The gauntlet of the glove must cover about half of the forearm to prevent the opponent's blade from entering the jacket sleeve.

Manner of Foil Fencing

Fencers may fence in their own styles as long as they observe the rules of fencing. These rules require that fencers compete in a courteous and honest manner. Dangerous actions, such as running into the opponent, falling, or otherwise fencing with lack of body control, are forbidden. Fencers may not reverse their body position allowing the back shoulder to move forward of the front shoulder. Fencers are required to keep their masks on until the referee calls "Halt."

Touching

The foil is a thrusting weapon only, and offensive actions must be made with the point, which must distinctly reach the target in order to be counted as a touch.

Target

The valid target for men and women is the torso from the collar to a horizontal line that joins the tops of the hip bones across the back, and to the groin line in front. The arms, from the shoulder seams outward, are excluded.

Off-Target Hits

When a point touches any part of the body other than the target, it is an off-target, or foul touch. It stops all action and no subsequent touch is allowed.

Handling the Weapon

The foil may be used with one hand only. A fencer may not switch hands during a bout unless the director gives special permission because of an injury.

Coming on Guard

The fencer whose name is called first should come on guard on the referee's right, unless the first person called is a left-handed fencer, in which case he should go to the referee's left.

Fencers are required to salute each other, the referee, and the audience before coming on guard. The bout is not ended until both fencers salute again in the same manner. Failure to salute is penalized by a Group 3 red card for a first offense, and a black card for a second offense (see penalty chart fig. 8.8).

Length of a Bout

In preliminary pools a bout lasts until one person has scored five touches, or until four minutes of fencing time have elapsed. In an elimination round, bouts are for fifteen touches, fenced in three, three minute periods with a one minute rest between periods. The timer stops the bout when time has run out.

Bouts are timed by a stopwatch or clock. The clock is started when the referee says "Fence," and the clock stops when the referee says "Halt."

In a five touch bout, if time is up before either fencer has scored five touches, an equal number of touches will be added to each fencer's score to bring the total of the larger score to 5. For instance, if time runs out with a score of 3–1, two points would be added to each score to make the official score 5–3. If a bout is tied at the end of the fencing period, the score will be advanced to 4–4 and fencers will continue, until the final point is won. Fencers may ask how much time remains at any time that the bout has been halted.

At the beginning of a bout, and after each score, fencers must start in the center of the width of the strip, with both feet behind their respective on-guard lines, which are 6 ft. 7 in. from the center line.

After fencers salute at the command "On guard," fencers come to the guard position. Then the referee asks, "Are you ready?" When both fencers reply in the affirmative, the referee begins the bout with the command, "Fence." If fencers do not respond when asked if they are ready, the referee will wait for a few seconds and again give the "Fence" command.

Beginning, Stopping, and Restarting a Bout

At the command "Fence," time is in, and either fencer may initiate the offensive. Once play begins, the contestants may stop only at their own risk until the bout is officially stopped by the command, "Halt."

Only the referee may halt the bout unless an unsafe situation arises, such as an injury or a broken blade; then a judge may halt the bout.

The referee stops the bout when a touch, valid or off-target, is made, when a fencer steps off of the strip with both feet, anytime a corps-à-corps or any other irregular play exists, whenever a judge raises a hand, or when, in the referee's opinion, the bout should be stopped for any other reason.

Fencing at Close Quarters

This is allowed as long as fencers are able to use their weapons correctly and the referee is able to follow the action.

Displacing the Target and Reversing Positions

Displacing the target and ducking are allowed, but reversing position or turning one's back or rear shoulder ahead of the front shoulder is not.

Ground Gained or Lost

When a bout is halted, each fencer must retreat equally in order to maintain fencing distance, with foil arms extended, points in line, and foil tips not touching. The following cases are exceptions to this rule: when a valid hit is scored, fencers are put on guard at equal distances at the center of the strip as they were at the beginning of the bout; when a bout stops because of a corps-á-corps, only the fencer who caused the clinch must give ground.

Stepping Off the Strip

Whenever a fencer steps off the strip with both feet, the referee must immediately call "Halt." If a fencer is touched while stepping off the strip, by an action that was already in motion when he or she stepped off the strip, the touch is awarded. Any touch made by a fencer who has stepped off the strip will not count.

Rear Limits of the Strip

If a competitor crosses the end line with both feet, a point is awarded to the other fencer. This rule eliminates the previous one-meter warning line. The current rule requires a two-meter visual warning line that is clearly marked, preferably in a different color.

A fencer may be put on guard behind the two-meter line without any warning other than the visual warning line.

Lateral Boundaries

When a fencer crosses a side line with both feet the penalty is 1 meter (3 ft. 3 in.). If this penalty places one over the end line with both feet, a touch will be awarded to the opponent.

Corps-á-Corps

Corps-á-corps exists when a fencer remains in body contact with an opponent so that correct fencing is not possible. When a fencer systematically causes a corps-á-corps, even without violence, that person is given a warning (yellow card, see penalty chart, fig. 8.8). When a fencer attacks with brutality, a black card should be given, causing expulsion from a meet.

Use of the Unarmed Hand

A fencer may not cover the target with the nonsword hand. A fencer may not grab the opponent's foil.

Evaluation Question

Which of the following actions result in a penalty for the fencer responsible: failure to salute the audience; ducking to avoid a touch; turning one's back to the opponent?

Officials

The Referee

The referee is completely in charge of the bout. Duties of the referee are to stop and start the bout, to make sure that all clothing and equipment are safe and legal, to supervise other officials, to maintain order, to penalize for faults, and to award touches.

The Jury

In an electrically scored meet the referee conducts the bouts. The referee may also ask for two side judges to watch for hand violations or hits made on the floor.

If a tournament is fenced with standard (nonelectric) weapons, the jury consists of a referee and four judges.

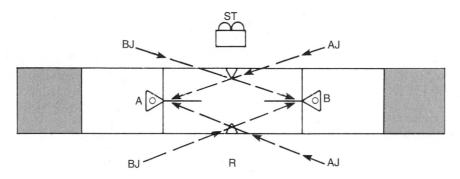

Figure 8.2
Placement of officials—standard foil. Fencer A (A), judges who watch fencer A (AJ), fencer B (B); judges who watch fencer B (BJ); referee (R); scorer (S); timer (T).

Nonelectric Meet Side Judges

With four judges, two stand on each side of the referee, one on each side of the strip, slightly behind the fencers. Each judge watches the fencer who is farther away, so that the two judges on the referee's right watch the fencer on the referee's left, and vice versa.

Judges watch for any point hits, valid or not, that land on the fencer they watch. When a judge sees a point land he or she must immediately signal the referee by raising a hand and the referee must then call "Halt."

Method of Determining Hits

The referee must briefly reconstruct the actions of the last phase before the halt and ask the appropriate judges whether a touch was made in the course of play.

A judge may respond by saying:

"Yes," a valid touch has been scored;
"Off target," a point has landed but is foul;
"No," no point landed, valid or off target;
"Abstain," no vote because action was blocked from vision.

The referee votes last and adds up the votes as follows:

one point for the vote of each judge;
one and one-half points for his or her own vote;
no points for an abstention.

If two judges on one side agree that a touch was valid, off target, or did not land, their decision must stand, even if the referee does not agree, because their two votes outweigh the referee's one and one-half votes.

If, on the other hand, one judge says "No" and the other says "Yes" or "Off target," the referee has the deciding vote.

If one judge says "Yes," "Off target," or "No," and the other abstains, the referee may overrule the judge who has voted, if there is disagreement.

If one judge answers "Yes" or "Off target," and the other answers, "No," and if the referee abstains, no point is awarded, but no later action may be awarded against the fencer who might have landed a hit. If the fencer who made a doubtful, valid touch then makes a definite touch without having been scored on, the touch must be awarded. In other words, a fencer who scores should not be penalized for a previous, possible touch that was not awarded.

Electric Meet Side Judges

When a meet is electrically scored but not fenced on a metal strip, two ground judges may be used. The judges stand on opposite sides of the referee, one at each end of the strip, and observe all actions. They determine whether a touch that registers as an off-target touch was made on the floor.

Two judges may also be used to watch for covering of the valid target with the nonfoil hand if the director thinks it is necessary to do so.

Scorer

The scorer marks points for the fencers who make a valid touch. He or she marks the score and announces the name and score of the person who scored, then announces the score of the other fencer. The scorer also calls fencers to the strip to fence and announces "on deck" bouts so that the next two to fence will be ready when their turn comes and no time will be lost in starting the next bout.

Timer

In an official meet a time limit is set on bouts. The timer uses a stopwatch or stopclock to keep track of actual fencing time only. Time is "in" from the referee's command of "Fence" to that of "Halt." In a five touch bout, when four minutes have passed, the timer ends the bout by ringing a bell or buzzer or by calling "Halt."

Fencers may ask how much time remains at any time the bout has been halted.

Officiating Techniques

At most fencing tournaments fencers are expected to be willing and able to assist with the officiating. Referees are, for the most part, amateur fencers who gladly give their time in the interest of fencing. It is desirable, therefore, that all fencers learn to officiate in any capacity so that they can assist in the running of meets and better understand and appreciate all aspects of the sport.

The United States Fencing Association ranks officials by means of examinations. Whenever possible, ranked referees should be used. They may receive payment for expenses incurred.

It takes experience to become a good referee or judge. These tasks require the entire attention of officials involved if they are to see and accurately explain actions that occur during a bout. The entire climate of a tournament is affected by the attitudes and abilities of the director and jury, who may either inspire confidence and establish a high level of efficiency, or through indecision, allow sloppy fencing or poor sportsmanship to lower the standard of fencing and morale of fencers and spectators alike.

Refereeing Techniques

The referee is a vital part of a tournament. He or she is responsible for, and has authority over, the actions of both fencers and spectators. He or she sets the standard and overall climate of the meet.

The referee must know the rules, but in case of a challenge or if an unusual situation arises, a rule book should be available. The referee's voice should be clear and authoritative so that the command of "Fence" and "Halt" may be heard clearly by both the fencers and the timer.

Starting the Bout

The referee must see that the fencers and officials are all in place before beginning the bout. When in place, and having saluted, they are asked, "Are you ready?" and, when the fencers reply in the affirmative, the referee says, "Fence."

Refereeing with a Jury

Since standard foils must often be used in classroom or fencing salle tournaments, it is necessary that fencers understand how to be an effective official in such instances.

The referee stands midway between fencers and about ten feet to the side in order to follow the action and still see the judges. The referee moves with the fencers at all times as the action moves up and down the strip. Besides allowing the referee to see action clearly, this central position simplifies the task of indicating the center of the field of play and keeps the director out of the judges' line of vision.

The referee allows play to continue until a point lands or any irregular fencing occurs, or if in the referee's opinion the bout should be stopped for any other reason.

A referee can upset the fencers by calling halt too often for no reason. As long as no point has landed and the fencing is not too confusing to follow, competitors should be allowed to continue. However, if there is cause, the bout should be halted immediately. If several actions take place after a point lands, it is more difficult to analyze play, so the call to halt must be issued immediately after a point arrives.

When action stops because of a possible touch, the referee should quickly give a résumé of the last phase. The referee is there to run a bout efficiently with a minimum of delays, not to put on an exhibition of knowledge or to overshadow the fencing with a performance. The referee is there only to facilitate fencing, and lengthy explanations of every detail of the bout may unduly delay the game.

After a brief description of the last phase, the referee should question the judges about the materiality of hits. The referee should follow the right-of-way sequence and determine whether the first attack landed. If it did and the right-of-way was clear, a point is awarded, and no further questions need to be asked. If the attack failed, the referee must find out which, if any, subsequent action landed and award touches according to these findings.

The referee should always give an opinion of materiality (did a point land?) last so as not to influence the responses of the judges in any way. One should not lead the judges with such questions as "Did you see the point land on the hand?" or "Do you agree that the point missed?" It would be better to ask, "Did the attack land?" a simple statement that does not suggest how the judge should answer.

Evaluation Question

Why should the referee's opinion of materiality be the last statement made by the referee?

Validity

If both fencers are hit, the referee alone is responsible for determining validity. He or she also may see points land, but it is more important to know the sequence of action. If two touches arrive at about the same time, the referee must decide which fencer had the right-of-way; if unable to determine which fencer was right, no touch may be awarded. If the referee determines that neither fencer clearly had right-of-way, a simultaneous touch is declared, and no touch is awarded.

Unfortunately, inconsistencies in determining right-of-way in competitive fencing are seen too often. It is important for a director to be consistent in deciding validity. Generally speaking, the attack is considered correct if two touches occur at about the same time. According to the 1991 Rules Book, Article 233:1,[1] "The simple attack . . . is correctly executed when the straightening of the arm with the point threatening the valid target precedes the beginning of the lunge or flèche." Article 233:2 further states that the arm must be extended during the first feint or during the advance of a composite attack. If the arm is not extended with the point in line as the rule requires, the attacker is vulnerable to an offensive action by the other fencer.

When a halt is called and no touch is awarded, the referee must indicate the center of the field of play so the fencers can properly position themselves when they are ready to resume action.

Judging Techniques

Each judge watches materiality of touches against the fencer who is farthest away. The judges are to assist the referee and are not in any way to try to dominate or delay the fencing.

A judge must move with the action to maintain a position just behind the nearest fencer and at the side of the strip. In this position judges will not obstruct the view of the referee or get in the way of the fencers, yet at least one of the two judges at each end of the strip will have a clear view of what happens. While the judges are not responsible for knowing who has the right-of-way, they must know how many actions were made against the fencer they are watching so that they will know which attempt touched when there has been a series of actions. It is to a judge's advantage to count actions as they occur in order to be able to say clearly whether it was the first, second, or fourth action that landed.

A judge must raise a hand instantly on seeing a point land, on or off target. If there is hesitation it will be more difficult to decide which action landed and time will be lost, so the hand must be raised quickly. The hand must also be raised high enough to be seen clearly out of the corner of the referee's eye. Conversely, the judge's hand must not be raised unless something is really seen. Nothing is more annoying to a fencer who has planned a series of actions that will lead to a touch than to have a judge who anticipated a touch stop action only to say, "No, I guess nothing really happened," or "I'm not sure."

When a referee asks a judge whether an action landed or not, this does not require a lengthy description of where and how the point went. A good judge abstains when not sure whether a point landed or not; an abstention may also be a weak, indecisive

Figure 8.3
An electrically scored foil bout. The referee, at the right edge of the illustration, is far enough from the fencers to be able to watch all of the action develop, and the scoring machine on the table to the left.

answer from a judge who is afraid to express an opinion for fear of being wrong. A judge must tell what is seen without being influenced by another judge's opinion or by comments or gestures from fencers or spectators. One must be sure to answer to the best of one's ability at all times, not just take the easy way out by refusing to vote.

Refereeing with Electrical Apparatus

The duties of the referee are the same whether a meet is electrically scored or not, but the means of deciding touches is different. When there are no judges to assume partial responsibility, the referee's task is perhaps even more demanding. Although the machine alone can determine if a point has been made, the referee must be aware of all of the action that takes place, and must also watch the scoring box in order to see when a light goes on.

The first task, at the start of each bout, is to see that all equipment is working properly before fencing begins, even though fencers are responsible for their own personal equipment. If a foil is not registering properly or there are any tears in an electric vest, they must be repaired or replaced.

Referee's Position

The referee should stand so that he or she can see the scoring lights as well as the action at all times. This means that, except when fencers are in the center of the strip, the referee will stand at one end of the action or the other in order to see both the fencers and the lights. If lights of both fencers have turned on, the referee must still be aware of who has the right-of-way to decide to whom the touch is awarded.

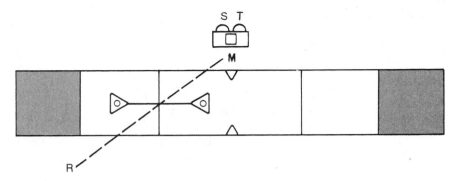

Figure 8.4
Placement of officials—electric foil. The referee (R) must maintain a position that permits vision of the scoring machine (M) as well as the fencers. S is the scorer; T is the timer.

How to Read the Scoring Lights

There are two lights for each fencer: a white light and a colored light. The bout must be stopped whenever a light and the buzzer go on. No touch may be awarded unless it has been registered by the machine.

If only a white light turns on, an off-target touch has been made against the fencer on whose side the light appears. If only a colored light registers, a valid touch was made against the fencer on whose side the light appears.

If lights appear on both sides, the referee must determine the validity and award the touch accordingly or declare a simultaneous touch with no score.

Only the apparatus may determine materiality of a touch. If, however, the director suspects that a touch was indicated when none occurred, he may disregard the point if the electric equipment is found to be faulty. No touch may be awarded unless it registers, even if a fault in the equipment is found.

General Rules for Determining the Validity of Touches

The referee alone decides on validity of touches in the event that both fencers are touched. The fencers may not question the referee's judgment about what occurred, but they may question the application of rules in view of what the referee and the judges say took place. The following are the basic right-of-way rules that must be used in determining validity, according to the 1991 USFA Rules Book, articles 233–236.[2]

"In order to judge the correctness of an attack, the following points must be considered:

233: 1. The simple attack, direct or indirect, is correctly executed when the straightening of the arm, the point threatening the valid target, precedes the initiation of the lunge or of the flèche;

2. The compound attack is correctly executed when the arm is straightened in the presentation of the first feint, with the point threatening the valid target, and the arm is not bent during the successive actions of the attack and the initiation of the lunge or of the flèche;
3. The attack with a step-forward-lunge or step-forward-flèche is correctly executed when the straightening of the arm precedes the end of the step forward and the initiation of the lunge or the flèche;
4. The simple or compound action executed with a bent arm, or a forward movement or feint executed with a bent arm, is not considered an attack, but rather a preparation that lays itself open to the initiation of the offensive or offensive/defensive action of the opponent;
5. If the attack is initiated when the opponent is not "in line," that is to say with the arm extended and the point threatening the valid target, it may be executed either with a direct thrust, or by a disengage, or by a cutover, or may even be preceded by a beat or successful feints obliging the opponent to parry.
6. If the attack is initiated when the opponent is "in line," that is to say with the arm straight and the point threatening the valid target, the attacker must, first, deflect the opponent's blade.
7. If the attacker, when attempting to deflect the opponent's blade, fails to find it, the right of attack passes to the opponent.
8. If the attack, the stop, or the feints are executed with the arm bent, the right-of-way passes to the opponent.

234: (b) The parry gives the right to riposte; the simple riposte may be direct or indirect, but to annul any subsequent action by the attacker, it must be executed immediately, without indecision or delay.

235: (c) When a compound attack is made, if the opponent finds the blade during one of the feints, the opponent gains the right to riposte.

236: (d) When compound attacks are made, the opponent has the right to stop thrust; but to be valid the stop thrust must arrive before the attacker has begun the final movement of the attack."

Scoring

Touches are recorded for the fencer who has scored, so that the fencer who first receives a score of five wins.

Scoring for Individual Meets

Individual meets are usually round-robin tournaments in which each fencer competes against every other person within the meet or pool. If more than ten fencers are competing, there must be a preliminary round or rounds consisting of two or more smaller pools. In championship tournaments, fifty percent or more of the competitors from each pool must advance. In class or intramural tournaments, however, the number of fencers per pool and the number who advance may be modified to suit the given situation.

NAME (Last & Init.)	No.	1	2	3	4	5	6	7	8	V	HS	–	HR	=	IND.	PL.
Simms, K	1	xxxx xxxx xxxx														
Brown, C	2		xxxx xxxx xxxx	111 / D												
Schultz, B	3		### / V	xxxx xxxx xxxx												
Jones, M	4				xxxx xxxx xxxx											
Maxx, J	5					xxxx xxxx xxxx										
Wilson, L	6						xxxx xxxx xxxx									
Marn, T	7							xxxx xxxx xxxx								
Richards, L	8								xxxx xxxx xxxx							

V = Victories; HS = Hits Scored; HR = Hits Received; HS–HR = Indicators.

First, count victories. If there is a tie, then count indicators.

Schultz (3) has a victory over Brown (2).

Figure 8.5
Round robin score sheet.

Order of Bouts.

The order of bouts in each pool is as follows:

Pool of 4 fencers	Pool of 5 fencers	Pool of 6 fencers	Pool of 7 fencers	Pool of 8 fencers		Pool of 9 fencers		Pool of 10 fencers	
1–4	1–2	1–2	1–4	2–3	8–5			1–4	3–8
2–3	3–4	4–5	2–5	1–5	7–2	1–9	3–1	6–9	4–9
1–3	5–1	2–3	3–6	7–4	1–3	2–8	2–4	2–5	6–5
2–4	2–3	5–6	7–1	6–8		3–7	5–9	7–10	10–2
3–4	5–4	3–1	5–4	1–2		4–6	8–6	3–1	8–1
1–2	1–3	6–4	2–3	3–4		1–5	7–1	8–6	7–4
	2–5	2–5	6–7	5–6		2–9	4–3	4–5	9–3
	4–1	1–4	5–1	8–7		8–3	5–2	9–10	2–6
	3–5	5–3	4–3	4–1		7–4	6–9	2–3	5–8
	4–2	1–6	6–2	5–2		6–5	8–7	7–8	4–10
		4–2	5–7	8–3		1–2	4–1	5–1	1–9
		3–6	3–1	6–7		9–3	5–3	10–6	3–7
		5–1	4–6	4–2		8–4	6–2	4–2	8–2
		3–4	7–2	8–1		7–5	9–7	9–7	6–4
		6–2	3–5	7–5		6–1	1–8	5–3	9–5
			1–6	3–6		3–2	4–5	10–8	10–3
			2–4	2–8		9–4	3–6	1–2	7–1
			7–3	5–4		5–8	2–7	6–7	4–8
			6–5	6–1		7–6	9–8	3–4	2–9
			1–2	3–7				8–9	3–6
			4–7	4–8				5–10	5–7
				2–6				1–6	1–10
				3–5				2–7	
				1–7					
				4–6					

Figure 8.6
Order of bouts for a round robin meet.
(Source: *Fencing Rules*. 1987 ed., p. 11.)

There is a specific "order of bouts" to be followed in a fencing meet (see fig. 8.6). When the correct order of bouts is followed and the pools consist of five or more people, no fencer will have to fence two consecutive bouts. In accordance with the example shown in figure 8.5, when there are eight fencers, their names are written in the first column. The first bout is between fencers two and three. The scorer announces it and then the next on deck bout, which is between fencers one and five. The scorer should draw a horizontal line through each frame of the bout in progress if a line does not already appear. To determine which frames to use, find the intersecting frame by reading across from fencer number one to the fourth frame. All touches for number one will be marked there. Likewise, read from fencer number four across to the coordinator of number one, and mark touches for number four in that frame. In short, read down to see who was touched and across to see by whom. In the example, figure 8.5, number three won, five to three. A V for victory or D for defeat is entered, and the next bout is called.

When all the bouts have been fenced, total victories and defeats are recorded in the columns to the right of the scores. The fencer with the most victories wins. In

No.	Name	Score		No.	Name	Score	
	SCHOOL				**SCHOOL**		
1.	Josephs	卌	V	1.	Alberts	‖	D
2.	Michaels	‖‖	D	2.	Fredericks	卌	V
3.	Johns	卌	V	3.	Thomas	‖	D
1.	Josephs	‖‖‖	D	2.	Fredericks	卌	V
2.	Michaels	卌	V	3.	Thomas	‖	D
3.	Johns	‖‖	D	1.	Alberts	卌	V
1.	Josephs	卌	V	3.	Thomas	Ø	D
2.	Michaels	Ø	D	1.	Alberts	卌	V
3.	Johns	卌	V	2.	Fredericks	‖‖	D
	Total Victories		5		Total Victories		4

Figure 8.7
Team score sheet.
(Source: *Fencing Rules.* 1982 ed., p. N–8.)

the event of a tie for first place, there is a fence-off to determine the winner. Indicators are used to determine all other places in the event of ties. The total of all touches given minus all touches received determines place. The greater the difference, the better the score (indicator).

Elimination Rounds

Large tournaments now consist of a combination of round-robin pools, followed by a double elimination, or a direct elimination final round. Qualifiers to the final round are seeded according to their round-robin results. It is important for competitors to do their best in the preliminary round in order to be seeded against weaker fencers in the elimination round.

Psychologically the elimination rounds are more demanding than round-robin pools because if you have one bout in which you are not at your best, you may be eliminated, or after two losing bouts in the case of a double-elimination format. In the round-robin format a fencer meets all fencers in a pool, allowing more fencing but also more chance for letting up just a bit and still perhaps winning if all other fencers also lose one or more bouts.

Team Scoring

A team may consist of three, four, or five men or women. International teams have four fencers, while most USFA teams consist of three. Collegiate teams sometimes have five members for dual meets, but it is probably more common to have three. In a team match, every fencer on one team fences every fencer on the other, so a match between two teams of three fencers each would consist of nine bouts. Sixteen bouts would be needed for a four-fencer team and twenty-five for a five-fencer team.

The NCAA rules manual contains a simplified method of recording scores for a team match.[3]

Scores should be announced after each touch is recorded so that the fencers and director can clearly hear them. If an error is made by the scorer, it must be corrected immediately because the score is official after the bout. Fencers can ask for a correction at the time a touch is made and recorded, but they can not protest the scoring of any previous point, so they should be aware of the score, as should the director.

Penalties

There are three classes of penalties:[4]

1. Warning, represented by a **Yellow Card.** Every further offense during that bout by the fencer thus warned will result in a penalty touch.
2. Penalty Touch, represented by a **Red Card.** One touch is added to the opponent's score; this can cause loss of the bout.
3. Exclusion From the Site of the Competition, represented by a **Black Card.**

On the following penalty chart (fig. 8.8), the letters "F," "E," "S" that appear in parentheses refer to Foil, Epee, or Sabre.

Notes

1. *Fencing Rules,* 1991 ed. (Colorado Springs, CO: United States Fencing Association, Inc.) 37ff.
2. *Fencing Rules,* 1991 ed., 33ff.
3. *Fencing Rules,* 1982 ed., N–8.
4. *Fencing Rules,* 1991 ed., Article 635.

7. The offenses and their penalties

OFFENSES	ARTICLES	Penalty Cards: 1st 2nd 3rd + Offense		
		1st call YC	**2nd call RC**	**3rd call BC**
Not present to fence on time (3 calls at 1 min intervals)[5]	604, 650			
First Group:				
Non-conforming equipment,[1] no spare regulation weapon	21, 27			
Voluntary corps-á-corps (and involuntary - F,S), jostling,	28, 34, 224	Y		
falling, disorderly fencing, reversing shoulders (F)[2]	318, 412	E		
Raising the mask before the referee's halt	28	L		
Covering or substitution of valid target (F,S)	30, 411	L	R	R
Using the non-weapon arm or hand[2]	30	O	E	E
Touching/holding the electrical equipment	30	W	D	D
Leaving the strip without permission	32			
Turning the back on the opponent[2]	35			
Crossing the side of the strip to avoid a touch	43	C	C	C
Delaying the bout	48	A	A	A
Placing the point of the weapon on the strip (F,E)	211, 316	R	R	R
Grounding the weapon on the lamé (F)[2]	230	D	D	D
Voluntary touch not on the opponent (F,E)	230, 325			
Touch scored with the guard (S)[2]	409			
Disobedience	602f., 606, 609			
Unjustified appeal	661			
Second Group:				
Absence of inspection marks[1,3]	21	R	R	R
Violent, dangerous or vindictive act, hit with guard or pommel[2]	28	E	E	E
Unjustified claim of injury[4]	50	D	D	D
Voluntary touch not on the opponent **in final minute** (F,E)	230, 325			
Third Group:				
Falsified inspection marks, modification of equipment[1,3,4,5]	21		B	
Dishonest fencing[2,5]	28	R	L	
Fencer disturbing order on the strip[5,8]	602	E	A	
Offense concerning publicity code[5]	PC	D	C	
Anyone disturbing order off the strip			K	
(1st: warning; 2nd: expulsion)[7,8]	602			
Fourth Group:				
Obvious fraud in the equipment[1,2,4,6]	21	B		
Intentional brutality[2,5]	28	L		
Unsportsmanlike conduct[2,5,6]	605	A		
Favoring the opponent, profiting from collusion[5]	607	C		
Doping[6]	608	K		

YELLOW = WARNING / RED = PENALTY TOUCH / BLACK = EXCLUSION

(1) Confiscation of non-conforming equipment
(2) Annulment of touch scored by fencer at fault
(3) Annulment of last touch scored by fencer at fault, even if fencing has recommenced
(4) Consult medical / technical experts
(5) Exclusion from the competition
(6) Exclusion from the tournament
(7) Expulsion from the sight of the competition
(8) In the most severe cases, the referee may exclude or expel the offender immediately

A fencer cannot receive a YELLOW CARD after receiving any RED CARD in the same bout. A fencer does not receive a 3rd group BLACK CARD without already having received a 3rd group RED CARD in that bout.

Figure 8.8
Penalty chart.

The Language of Fencing— A Glossary

9

Most fencing terms describe the actions to which they refer. Many of the terms in common usage in this country reflect the French or Italian origins of fencing, and although much of its terminology has been adapted or translated to English, many words are European. All international fencing championships are conducted in French, which is the international language of fencing, so the French influence predominates in terminology. Any serious student of fencing should become familiar with the fencing vocabulary.

Absence of the Blade
When the blades are not engaged.

Abstain
A judge may "abstain" or decline to vote if he or she was unable to see whether or not a point was made.

Advance
To move forward in the guard position.

Amateur Fencers League of America (AFLA)
This was the governing body of amateur fencing in the United States from 1891 until 1982.

Attack
An attempt to hit the opponent.

Attack on Preparation
An attack that is made as the opponent makes a beat, change, feint, or advance in preparation for his attack. This attack must begin before the opponent's attack actually begins.

Attack on the Blade
An action, such as a beat, press, or bind, that removes the opponent's blade from line to clear the way for an attack.

Ballestra
A jump-lunge attack. This term suggests the historic link between fencing and the formal ballet, which is said to have been influenced by the fencing positions.

Barrage
A fence-off of a tie between two or more fencers.

Beat
A sharp tap against the opponent's blade to clear the way for an offensive action.

Bind (Liément)

An action that removes a threatening blade by binding it, or carrying it from high line to the opposite low line by crossing the blade over the opponent's blade to hit in the low line with opposition. If the bind is executed vigorously enough, it may be used to disarm an opponent. Disarming an opponent, however, is no longer advantageous since action stops whenever a weapon is dropped. In the days of dueling and of early fencing, this was a valuable trick to master. Today it is a useful action, but no attempt is made to actually disarm a fencer by this means.

Call

A signal to stop the bout. If a fencer wishes to stop during a bout without danger of being hit, he or she may "call" to the referee to stop the bout by quickly stamping his or her forward foot two times.

Ceding Parry

A parry that gives against the opponent's blade.

Change Beat

A beat made by changing to a different line.

Change of Engagement

The act of going from one line to engage the blade in another.

Closed Line

A line that is protected by the blade and arm.

Compound Attack

Any attack consisting of two or more actions. It also may be called a composed attack.

Corps-á-Corps (Clinch)

Literally body-to-body, in which there is body contact or a closing of the guards so that normal fencing actions become impossible.

Coule (Glide)

A preparatory action that is made by gliding along the side of the opponent's blade.

Counter Attack

A stop thrust in which the time is taken from the attacker by touching before the final action of the original attack begins.

Counter Coupé

A simple cut-over that deceives the opponent's change of engagement.

Counter–Disengage

A simple disengage that deceives the opponent's change of engagement.

Counter Parry

A circular parry that is made by parrying in the side opposite the one to which an attack is made.

Counter Riposte

An offensive action that follows the successful parry of a riposte.

Counter Time

A second-intention attack.

Coupé

A cutover.

Cutover
A simple attack to a high line, made by passing the blade over the opponent's blade to hit on the other side of the blade.

Derobement (Deception)
An evasion of the opponent's attempt to engage or beat the blade.

Direct
Indicates that an attack or parry is made without changing lines.

Disengage
A simple attack that is made by passing under the opponet's blade to hit in another line.

Doublé
A compound attack in which the attacker feints a disengage and deceives a counter parry. This may be described as a corkscrew attack, or circular attack.

Double Change
Two quick changes of engagement, made without moving the hand laterally.

Double Disengage
A compound attack made by disengaging to deceive a counter parry, and a second disengage to deceive a lateral parry.

Engagement
The contact of two opposing blades.

Envelopment
A double bind that envelops the opposing, menacing blade in one motion that carries it in a complete circle to land in the original line.

Epee
A thrusting weapon in which the entire body is the target.

False Attack
A lunge made without the intention of landing in order to draw a response from the opponent.

Flying Parry-Riposte
This is a coupé parry-riposte that is made in one quick motion.

Federation Internationale d'Escrime (FIE)
The governing body of all international fencing tournaments. This organization was founded in Europe in the latter part of the nineteenth century, at which time some rules were set up to govern tournaments.

Feeble
The flexible or point third, of the blade.

Feint
A pretend attack that is made by a menacing extension of the foil arm. It is made preparatory to an attack in order to draw a response.

Fencing Time
The time required to make one simple fencing action. This time will vary according to the speed of the fencers in question.

Flèche

A running attack. The literal translation from the French is "arrow," which aptly describes this as a swift, flying attack.

Forte

The strong third of the blade that extends from the guard.

Glide

A straight attack, made by sliding along the opponent's blade.

Lines

The four theoretical areas of the target: upper inside and outside, and lower inside and outside.

Lunge

An extension of the guard position made in order to reach the opponent. The lunge was introduced during the last part of the sixteenth century as a new secret form of attack.

Mask

The protective wire helmet that is worn on the head. The first masks were made from sheet metal with eye slits cut out of them. These were never widely used because they were uncomfortable and very dangerous—the eye was vulnerable to hits because the metal allowed the point to slide to the eye slits. Some right-of-way conventions of fencing stem from the premask days when, for instance, it was considered wrong to riposte until the opponent had recovered from the lunge because to do so would have been extremely hazardous. The first wire masks were used around 1800.

Match

A contest between two teams.

Off-Target Hit

A point hit that does not land on the valid target. This term is now preferred to the term *foul*.

On Guard

The basic ready fencing position.

One-Two

A compound attack that consists of feinting a disengage and then disengaging to deceive a direct parry.

Parry

A defensive action that deflects the attacker's blade.

Passe

When the foil point grazes the target rather than hits it squarely.

Phrase or Phrase D'Armes

A period of continuous fencing that may consist of many actions by one or both fencers. When there is any break in play, a phrase ends.

Piste (Strip)

From the French word meaning "path." This is the fencing area. It may be said to resemble a path or strip because of its long, narrow shape.

Pommel
The metal part at the end of the handle that fastens the parts of the foil together and also acts as a counterweight to the blade, thereby making it a balanced weapon with a French handle.

President (Referee)
The individual who presides over a fencing meet.

Pressure
A preliminary motion made by applying a slight pressure against the opponent's blade to cause a reaction that will open the way for an attack.

Prise-de-Fer
A taking of the opponent's blade. This refers to a blade contact.

Redoublement
A new offensive action made against a fencer who defends without riposting.

Referee
The person in charge of a bout.

Remise
An immediate continuation of an attack that was parried or fell short. It is made without withdrawing the arm, usually while in a lunge.

Reprise
A new attack made after returning to the guard position.

Right-of-Way
The right to attack. It goes to the fencer who first extends the foil arm, or initiates an attack, or who parries an attack.

Riposte
An answering attack made by a fencer after he or she has successfully defended himself or herself.

Salute
An acknowledgment to an opponent, referee, and spectators, made with the blade. A fencer is required to salute before and at the end of a bout.

Second-Intention (Counter-Time) Attack
A false attack intended to draw a parry riposte that the original attacker then parries so he or she can hit on a counter riposte. The attacker intends throughout the action to hit on his or her second attack.

Semicircular Parry
A parry from high to low line or vice versa, so called because the point travels in an arc to make the parry.

Simple Attack
An attack consisting of just one motion. There are three simple attacks: straight thrust, disengage, and cutover.

Stop Thrust
A counter attack made by extending into a poorly executed attack. In order to be valid, a stop must arrive before the final motion of the attack begins.

Straight Thrust

A direct, simple attack that consists of a lunge to hit without changing the line of engagement.

Strip (Piste)

The field of play. The strip is usually made of rubber so that fencers will not slip as they move. In an electric fencing meet, the strip may be covered with wire mesh that grounds any hits to the floor that would otherwise register as off target.

Thrust

The action of hitting with an extended arm. To make a firm thrust the point is placed on the target with the action of the fingers.

Touch

A valid point hit against the opponent.

United States Fencing Association

The governing body of fencing in this country, renamed in 1982; formerly the Amateur Fencers League of America.

United States Fencing Coaches Association

The official coaches organization of this country.

Valid Touch

A point hit that lands on the target area without having first landed off target.

Suggested References

Fencing Rules: Authorized English Translation of the International Rules. Adopted by the United States Fencing Association and the National Collegiate Athletic Association. Colorado Springs, CO, 1991.

Glossary of Fencing Terms. United States Fencing Coaches Association. NJ 1995.

Questions

Multiple Choice

1. Fencing began to develop as a sport after
   a. dueling was outlawed.
   b. archers' accuracy with the bow and arrow made swordfighting obsolete.
   c. gunpowder came into common use.
   d. a duel in which a powerful French nobleman was killed by a sword.
2. Which modern fencing weapon most closely resembles real dueling?
   a. foil
   b. epee
   c. sabre
   d. rapier
3. Which weapon was designed as a practice weapon?
   a. foil
   b. epee
   c. sabre
   d. foil and epee
4. With which weapon(s) may "cuts" be made?
   a. foil
   b. epee
   c. sabre
   d. epee and sabre
5. Which of the following is **not** a part of the foil?
   a. points d'arret
   b. pommel
   c. tang
   d. bell
6. The governing body of fencing in this country is the
   a. AFCC.
   b. USFA.
   c. AAF.
   d. FIE.
7. Breakage of foil blades may be kept at a minimum by
   a. using very stiff blades.
   b. hitting squarely so that the blade will not bend.
   c. replacing blades every month.
   d. allowing the hand to "give upwards" so the blade will bend up.
8. When in the on-guard position, the proper distance between the heels is
   a. about shoulder width.
   b. about two feet.
   c. about one foot.
   d. the most natural stance.
9. The advance is made by
   a. moving first the back foot and then the front foot forward one step.
   b. moving both feet forward simultaneously.
   c. moving the front foot first and then the back foot.
   d. rocking the weight forward before stepping.
10. In an effective lunge, the rear leg is extended
    a. to lower the center of gravity.
    b. to provide force for the lunge.
    c. for aesthetic reasons.
    d. to complete the lunge.

11. When in the lunge, the body should
    a. lean forward as far as possible.
    b. not lean at all.
    c. remain balanced behind the forward leg.
    d. extend as far as possible.
12. The foil should be held
    a. loosely at all times.
    b. by the thumb and forefinger.
    c. tightly so it cannot be parried out of line.
    d. in a firm, yet relaxed grip.
13. In the relaxed guard position, the elbow of the sword arm should
    a. be tucked against the rib cage.
    b. project beyond the outline of the body as viewed by the opponent.
    c. be a hand's breadth from the body.
    d. be "broken" just enough to keep the sword arm from rigidity.
14. A balanced guard position permits the fencer to
    a. retreat more easily than advance.
    b. advance more easily than retreat.
    c. retreat or advance with equal ease.
    d. attack more easily than defend.
15. While in the guard position
    a. the hand is always kept to the left of the body for protection.
    b. the point is as high as the top of the opponent's mask.
    c. the hand moves left or right as necessary to protect any line.
    d. the hand remains stationary.
16. When in a full lunge, the forward knee should be
    a. in front of the toes.   c. over the instep.
    b. over the toes.   d. behind the heel.
17. When two fencers fence with feebles of their blades in contact, the blades are
    a. engaged.   c. on guard.
    b. disengaged.   d. in fourth position.
18. Correct fencing distance is
    a. with the points touching.
    b. close enough to eliminate the necessity of lunging.
    c. determined by the lunging distance of the shorter fencer.
    d. determined by the lunging distance of the taller fencer.
19. A "jump-lunge" is called a
    a. passata sotto.
    b. advance-lunge.
    c. flèche.
    d. ballestra.
20. The act of moving from six to engage the blade in four is called
    a. disengage.   c. change of engagement.
    b. double-change.   d. cutover.
21. In a simple attack, it is important to aim
    a. before extending the arm.   c. during the lunge.
    b. during the arm extension.   d. as you hit.

22. The three simple attacks are
    a. change of engagement, disengage, coupé.
    b. beat-coupé, beat-straight thrust, disengage.
    c. straight thrust, disengage, coupé.
    d. disengage, coupé, one-two.
23. Which of the following is a simple attack?
    a. beat-straight thrust
    b. coupé
    c. one-two
    d. doublé
24. The feint is
    a. a parry.
    b. an attack.
    c. a pretended attack.
    d. a false attack.
25. In a feint, the arm is
    a. not extended.
    b. extended.
    c. not fully extended.
    d. in the guard position.
26. A compound attack is
    a. preceded by an advance.
    b. always preceded by a beat.
    c. the same as a riposte.
    d. any attack of two or more actions.
27. A beat may properly be used
    a. to clear the opponent's blade away before an attack.
    b. to get the opponent to react, creating an opening for an attack.
    c. to upset an opponent who is obviously getting set to attack.
    d. any of the above.
28. The one-two
    a. starts with a beat.
    b. is a feint of disengage and a disengage.
    c. is a feint of disengage to avoid a parry.
    d. is a feint of disengage and a counter disengage.
29. The doublé is
    a. a simple attack.
    b. a feint of disengage.
    c. the avoiding of two direct parries.
    d. a feint of disengage and a disengage that avoids a circle parry.
30. An attack to the blade that is made only against an extended arm is a
    a. bind.
    b. glide.
    c. press.
    d. disengage.
31. The press is
    a. a preparatory action.
    b. the same as a beat.
    c. an attack.
    d. a glide.
32. The glide may effectively be used against a fencer who
    a. has a heavy hand.
    b. has a light hand.
    c. fences with absence of the blade.
    d. changes engagement often.
33. Advance-attacks should **not** be used against
    a. a fencer who has a longer reach than you.
    b. a fencer who can be relied on to retreat as you attack.
    c. a fencer who stands his or her ground when parrying.
    d. any of the above.

34. The flèche is
    a. a running attack.
    b. a lunging attack.
    c. an illegal attack.
    d. a corps-á-corps.
35. The flèche should
    a. not be used in foil.
    b. never be used.
    c. be used sparingly.
    d. be used in preference to the lunge whenever an opponent can be counted on to retreat with the parry.
36. The parry is
    a. a defensive action.
    b. either offensive or defensive.
    c. an offensive action.
    d. any beat.
37. The inside lines are
    a. four and six.
    b. four and seven.
    c. six and eight.
    d. six and seven.
38. Semicircular parries are made when
    a. moving from a guard of six to parry in four.
    b. taking a high line, circular parry.
    c. taking a low line, circular parry.
    d. moving from high line to parry in low line or vice versa.
39. If an attacker's arm withdraws during the attack,
    a. it does not count, even though it lands.
    b. it still has the right-of-way.
    c. the opponent may extend and take right-of-way.
    d. it is called a foul touch.
40. The stop-hit
    a. is illegal.
    b. is usually dangerous.
    c. should be made against a simple attack.
    d. should be used only against a cutover.
41. When an opponent retreats at each of your attacks, you may effectively
    a. wait for the person to advance, attacking into the advance.
    b. gain ground and attack with a lunge again.
    c. make a ballestra attack.
    d. any of the above.
42. If an attack fails, the attacker should
    a. continue play until a point lands.
    b. retreat.
    c. return to the guard position and engage blades before continuing.
    d. close in to stop action.
43. If an opponent makes a fast disengage, it would usually be best to
    a. retreat.
    b. advance.
    c. parry and riposte.
    d. make a stop thrust.
44. If an opponent is very aggressive, making many composed attacks, it would be effective for a fencer to
    a. wait for the attack and make a parry riposte to score.
    b. parry, but not riposte.
    c. extend into the attack and hope to land first.
    d. attack in an attempt to confuse the opponent.

45. In a regulation women's bout, the winner must score
    a. five touches.
    b. the most out of a total of ten touches.
    c. four touches.
    d. all she can in four minutes of fencing time.
46. The valid foil target excludes
    a. the head and arms.   c. the left side.
    b. the back.   d. the head.
47. The riposte
    a. has right-of-way over an attack.
    b. is an attack made by the defender after parrying an attack.
    c. is a continuation of an attack after failing to land.
    d. is not valid unless it is made with a lunge.
48. If an off-target hit is made,
    a. it is a touch against the attacker.
    b. it is a touch against the defender.
    c. it stops all action immediately.
    d. fencers stop and go to the center of the strip.
49. When a valid touch is made,
    a. fencers cross blades and resume action where they stopped.
    b. fencers must stop and resume action in the center of the strip.
    c. if there is a referee, the one who scored the touch stops and waits for the
       referee to acknowledge the point.
    d. if there is a referee, the fencer who is hit must stop and acknowledge being hit.
50. The foil strip is
    a. 6'7" by 46'.   c. 4' by 20'.
    b. 6'7" by 60'.   d. 4' by 46'.
51. When a fencer backs off the end of the strip with both feet,
    a. a touch is awarded to the other fencer.
    b. fencers are stopped and brought in two meters.
    c. a touch is awarded unless it occurs on the last touch.
    d. the bout continues until a touch is made.
52. In an official, standard foil bout,
    a. the referee may overrule all four judges.
    b. the referee may overrule one judge because he or she has 1 1/2 votes to 1
       vote for each judge.
    c. the judges must watch right-of-way as well as touches.
    d. the referee has no vote but watches for validity of touches.
53. In an official, standard foil bout,
    a. judges must call out whenever they see a point land.
    b. only the referee may officially stop the bout, except in an emergency or
       when time runs out.
    c. fencers are obliged to call touches received.
    d. fencers should stop fencing if a point lands, called or not.
54. A bout is not stopped
    a. for an invalid touch.
    b. when a blade slaps or grazes a target.
    c. when a fencer goes off the strip.
    d. when a corps-á-corps exists.

55. This score sheet indicates that

	1	2	3	4
1			Ⅲ	
2				ⅤⅠ
3	Ⅱ			
4		Ⅱ		

    a. No. 2 defeated No. 1.
    b. No. 2 defeated No. 4.
    c. No. 4 defeated No. 1.
    d. No. 4 defeated No. 2.

56. In the bout between fencers 1 and 3, on the same score sheet, time has run out. The score will be
    a. 2–3, No. 3 wins.
    b. advanced to 5–2, No. 1 wins.
    c. advanced to 5–4, No. 1 wins.
    d. as it stands at 2–3 with a double loss.

57. Fencers are required to wear an underarm protector that must
    a. be sewn into the jacket.
    b. have at least four layers of heavy material.
    c. have no armpit seam.
    d. have two sleeves.

58. A foil glove
    a. is optional clothing.
    b. must extend over the lower part of the jacket sleeve.
    c. may be of any durable material.
    d. must be heavily padded.

59. Mental practice is considered to be
    a. of questionable value.
    b. detrimental to performance on an advanced level.
    c. better than actual physical practice.
    d. of value.

60. Stretching exercises are beneficial for fencers because they
    a. may help to prevent injury.
    b. act to "psych" up a fencer.
    c. increase strength of the leg muscles.
    d. increase cardiorespiratory capacity.

True or False

61. Rules require fencers to salute before and after a bout.
62. Electrical scoring was developed primarily for spectator appeal.
63. The ballestra is a salute that derives from ballet.
64. The lunge should be preceded by an extended arm.
65. It is not possible to "overlunge."
66. Correct fencing distance is determined by lunging distance.
67. Passing the point underneath the opponent's blade to engage it on the other side is a disengage.
68. The upper outside line is six.
69. A parry may be made by beat or by opposition.
70. There are eight common parries in foil fencing.
71. The bind should be used only against an opponent who has an extended arm.
72. The flèche is most often used against an opponent who is out of distance.
73. A false attack is against the rules.
74. A riposte has right-of-way over a reprise.

75. If an attack lands off target and an immediate riposte hits the valid target, the riposte scores a touch.
76. If an attacker lands off target, then immediately lands on the valid target, the point shall be awarded.
77. A fencer may gain right-of-way by extending the foil arm, point in line, or by advancing.
78. If your opponent reacts to a feint of disengage with a counter parry, you may score by making a double.
79. A second-intent attack is an effective tactic against an opponent who makes stop thrusts.
80. An attack on preparation is a form of stop thrust.
81. An attack on preparation may take advantage of an opponent's pattern of lateral blade movements.
82. The valid foil target is the same for men and women.
83. The back is not a valid target.
84. A fencer may not switch hands during a bout unless given permission by the referee because of an injury to the favored hand.
85. A corps-á-corps exists whenever fencers remain in bodily contact.
86. Fencing at close quarters is allowed as long as weapons can be used correctly.
87. An off-target touch is the same as a flat touch.
88. A bout should be stopped when the point grazes the target.
89. If a point lands on the valid target, then bounces off, no touch is awarded.
90. If the back hand is hit while it covers any part of the valid target, a touch is awarded to the attacker.
91. After one warning, if a fencer again covers the valid target with the unarmed hand, a touch should be awarded to the opponent.
92. If two people attack at the same time with straight arms and both land at the same time, both are awarded a touch.
92. If an attack is parried and the defender does not riposte, the attacker may try to score again from the lunge position.
94. The riposte may be made only from the guard position.
95. A stop-hit into a continuous one-two attack does not take right-of-way.
96. A remise has right-of-way over an immediate riposte.
97. When a fencer steps off the side of the strip with both feet, and when no touch is made, the penalty is one meter.
98. Displacing the target by ducking is not allowed.
99. The referee of a bout is responsible for determining validity when both fencers are hit.
100. When fencing is stopped and no touch is made, fencers are put on guard, with blades engaged, where action stopped.

Foil Fencing

```
H  S  R  D  H  M  A  J  O  F  H  A  Q  H  K  K  O  F  L  L
C  V  E  E  T  A  R  G  E  T  M  R  F  F  O  I  L  C  W  S
T  E  M  F  L  N  U  R  J  D  A  U  C  E  W  I  N  N  X  L
F  T  I  E  R  G  Y  K  X  D  S  Q  N  I  C  F  L  U  F  D
L  A  S  N  S  T  R  I  P  N  K  E  E  N  R  O  P  H  J  I
E  C  E  D  C  O  U  P  E  R  I  G  H  T  O  F  W  A  Y  S
C  T  R  E  T  R  E  A  T  T  A  C  K  R  I  E  R  L  Q  E
H  I  P  R  B  L  A  D  E  P  R  E  S  S  S  N  I  N  K  N
E  C  P  L  A  Y  N  F  L  E  G  A  L  F  E  G  P  H  Y  G
I  J  Z  N  I  T  B  I  L  Q  D  T  H  X  R  A  O  S  B  A
C  S  O  K  L  Z  Y  N  O  Y  D  O  S  E  W  G  S  R  W  G
C  S  A  L  U  T  E  G  E  N  W  U  E  E  H  E  T  F  T  E
B  U  C  P  R  T  I  E  B  I  V  N  B  X  K  M  E  E  O  N
T  H  R  U  S  T  V  R  L  Y  C  P  O  M  M  E  L  E  U  Q
S  W  O  F  F  I  C  I  A  L  O  X  U  B  A  N  L  B  C  Z
Q  B  U  X  J  J  X  N  D  N  U  M  T  E  M  T  U  L  H  P
O  T  X  N  F  J  L  G  E  O  N  G  U  A  R  D  N  E  K  A
I  E  S  A  B  R  E  L  P  L  T  S  B  T  L  V  G  K  Q  R
G  I  M  L  L  D  O  L  E  E  E  Q  C  N  A  J  E  O  Z  R
J  C  E  W  F  S  T  F  E  V  R  U  E  P  G  Y  D  M  L  Y
```

There are 36 terms here related to fencing. Can you find them?

Index